The Market Shock

Published by the Austrian Academy of Sciences/
Research Unit for Socio-Economics

Distributed by the University of Michigan Press, Ann Arbor

Library of Congress Cataloguing-in-Publication Data applied for

ISBN 0-472-08204-3

Layout and Production by Patricia Blaas, Vienna
Jacket by Angela Dobrick, Hamburg

Printed by remaprint, Vienna

"*the pursuit of self-interest unrestrained by suitable institutions, carries no guarantee of anything except chaos*" - Lord Robbins

"*Natura non facit saltum*" - Alfred Marshall

"*permanent relations between debtors and creditors ... form the ultimate foundation of capitalism*" - J.M. Keynes

The Market Shock

An AGENDA for Socio-Economic Reconstruction of Central and Eastern Europe

edited by

Jan Kregel, Egon Matzner and Gernot Grabher
for the AGENDA-Group

This document was prepared with the support of scholars from
Austrian Academy of Sciences, Vienna: Institute of Demography and Research Unit for Socio-Economics * Austrian Institute of Economic Research, Vienna * Czechoslovak Academy of Sciences, Prague: Institute for Forecasting * Free University, Berlin: Institute for Economic Policy * Harvard University, Cambridge, Ma.: Law School * Hungarian Ministry of Finance, Budapest: Institute for Economic Policy and Planning * Institute for Security and Co-operation in Europe, Berlin * International Institute for Peace, Vienna * Jawaharlal Nehru University, New Delhi * Polish Institute of International Affairs, Warsaw * Russian Academy of Sciences, Moscow: Institute of Europe and Institute of World Economy and International Relations * Science Centre for Social Research (WZB), Berlin: Research Area Labour Market and Employment * The Vienna Institute for Comparative Economic Studies * Università degli Studi di Bologna: Dipartimento di Scienze Economiche * University of Bremen: Department of Economics * University of Ljubljana: Department of Economics * Vienna University of Technology: Institute of Public Finance.

CONTENTS page

PREFACE

Motivation

It is becoming increasingly apparent that the transformation of the formerly centrally planned economies of Central and Eastern Europe to free market economic systems is on the wrong track. The problem is not the ultimate goal of the transformation process, i.e. to establish economic activity on the basis of free market forces, but rather the fact that the transformation programmes currently being experimented appear to be causing avoidable human suffering without making appreciable progress towards creating viable domestic production and employment. AGENDA is the result of a series of discussions amongst a wide range of scholars who share the view that the transformation programmes which have been introduced since 1989 have severe deficiencies. In addition, all of the contributors are convinced that it would be unprincipled not to express concern about the dangers inherent in the present course of events.

Purpose

The purpose of AGENDA is to express scholarly concern about the deficiencies of current transformation programmes and to suggest positive measures to provide a better foundation for the socio-economic reconstruction of the former communist countries in Central and East Europe. The AGENDA is proposed as a check list for the evaluation and definition of more adequate transformation programmes. It is based on the belief that there is nothing in the currently implemented policies and the human discomfort that they have engendered that is inherent or even inevitable to a successful transition process. It is not meant to suggest that pain and hard work will not be part of a successful transformation process, but rather that waste and deprivation are part of a way of life that is inimical to the development of free market democracies. By drawing attention to possible alternatives it is hoped that present attitudes may be influenced before the pressure of events caused by current policies takes the upper hand and leads to unpredictable political outcomes.

Process

The idea for an AGENDA was first discussed by Amit Bhaduri and Egon Matzner in May 1991. At their invitation a group of scholars (see The AGENDA-Group, p. 9) gathered from 7 to 9 October 1991 at the Austrian Academy of Sciences in Vienna to discuss the main issues of the transformation process on the basis of more than a dozen of papers which were specially written for the meeting (see Appendix, Documentation of Background Papers). On the basis of these papers an initial draft of the AGENDA was drawn up by Egon Matzner. A revision was undertaken at the WZB in Berlin from 14 to 17 February 1992 by a Drafting Commission consisting of Amit Bhaduri, Jan Kregel, Egon Matzner, Leo Specht and Roberto M. Unger. The resulting draft was circulated for criticism and comments and the final draft completed during Easter 1992.

AGENDA would not have been possible without the support of three institutions: The Austrian Academy of Sciences, whose Research Unit for Socio-Economics sponsored the Workshop in Vienna in October 1991, the International Institute for Peace, Vienna which also participated in financial and administrative responsibilities of the Workshop and the Documentation of the work, and the Labour Market and Employment Research Unit of the

Science Centre for Social Research (WZB) which sponsored the meeting of the Drafting Committee in February 1992 in Berlin. Finally, the contributions of the participants in the Workshop provided an impetus without which AGENDA could not have been completed. A selection of contributions is planned to be published.

By its motivation, purpose and process, AGENDA documents its co-operative origin. It is the result of many ideas which were developed by the participants in the discussion and drafting stages. For this reason it would be inappropriate to assign individual responsibility for the final version, although the members of the Drafting Committee accept full responsibility for the selection and presentation of arguments which form the final version of AGENDA.

AGENDA was first presented to the public in Press Conferences in Prague on 24 May and in Vienna on 25 May 1992; it was subsequently presented to a Hungarian audience in Budapest on 8 September 1992. As a result of strong interest in the practical and scientific implications of the arguments contained in the document, the sponsoring institutions have decided to support its formal publication. The English language version is published by the Austrian Academy of Sciences, Research Unit for Socio-Economics with the financial support of the International Institue for Peace, Vienna and is distributed by

Michigan University Press. In addition to the English version, there will be a simultaneous publication in German sponsored by the Science Centre Berlin (Wissenschaftszentrum Berlin) and published by edition sigma, Berlin. A Ucranian version sponsored by the government in Kiev for educational purposes is also planned.

At the initiative of Erwin Lanc, President of the International Institute for Peace, Vienna, the summary of the basic arguments of AGENDA (chapter 7) has been made available in Czech, French, Hungarian, Polish, Russian, Serbian, Slovak, Slovenian and Spanish. Summaries have also appeared in international publications such as Challenge (New York), Die Zeit (Hamburg), Ekonomisk Revy (Belgrad) and Prace (Prague).

Since the document started as a discussion group and has passed through several drafting stages, it reflects the contributions of many individual points of view and some internal inconsistencies may still remain. Jan Kregel, Egon Matzner and Gernot Grabher have shared the editorial and scientific efforts of producing a coherent final draft; they have attempted to act as trustees of the ideas contributed at various stages of the discussion and drafting process but nevertheless accept full responsibility for the final form and content of the document. Patricia Blaas managed the editorial production and layout which allowed the transformation of the manuscript into printed form.

It is hoped that the publication of AGENDA will enhance the process of successful socio-economic transformation of the Eastern and Central European economies by focussing attention on those elements that the AGENDA-group considers to be essential to taking the 'shock' out of the introduction of the market.

Vienna, August 1992

Jan Kregel,
Egon Matzner,
Gernot Grabher

THE AGENDA-GROUP

Participants:

Dr. Laszlo ASZTALOS, Ministry of Finance, Budapest

Dr. Kurt BAYER, Austrian Institute of Economic Research, Vienna

Prof. Amit BHADURI, Indian Institute of Management, Calcutta

Dr. Gernot GRABHER, Science Centre Berlin for Social Research (WZB), Berlin

Dr. Hansjörg HERR, Science Centre Berlin for Social Research (WZB), Berlin

Prof. Dr. Peter KALMBACH, Bremen University, Bremen

Prof. Dr. Eveline KOLLOCH, Institut für Sicherheit und Zusammenarbeit in Europa, Berlin

Prof. Ing. Valtr KOMAREK, Institute for Forecasting, Chairman of the Foreign Policy Committee of the National Assembly, Praha

Prof. Jan KREGEL, University of Bologna and John´s Hopkins University Center, Bologna

Erwin LANC, former federal minister, International Institute for Peace, Vienna

Prof. Kazimierz LASKI, The Vienna Institute for Comparative Economic Studies, Vienna

Dr. Andrei S. LUSHIN, Institute of World Economy and International Relations, Russian Academy of Sciences, Moscow

Prof. Dr. Egon MATZNER, Institute of Public Finance, University of Technology, Vienna, Science Centre Berlin for Social Research (WZB), Berlin and Research Unit for Socio-Economics, Austrian Academy of Sciences, Vienna

Dr. Joze MENZINGER, TRG/Prawna fakultete, Ljubljana

Doz. Dr. Rainer MÜNZ, Institute of Demography, Austrian Academy of Sciences, Vienna

Prof. Dr. Maciej PERCZYNSKI, Polish Institute of International Affairs, Warsaw

Prof. emeritus Dr. K. W. ROTHSCHILD, University of Linz and Vienna

Prof. Dr. Max SCHMIDT, International Institute for Peace, Berlin

Dr. Victor L. SHEINIS, Institute of World Economy and International Relations, Russian Academy of Sciences, Moscow

Dr. Peter SINT, Research Unit for Socio-Economics, Austrian Academy of Sciences, Vienna

Dr. Swetlana A. SMIRNOWA, Institute of World Economy and International Relations, Russian Academy of Sciences, Moscow

Dr. Leo SPECHT, Law School, Harvard University, Cambridge, Ma. and Vienna

Mag. Peter STANIA, International Institute for Peace, Vienna

Prof. Josef STEINDL, Vienna

Mag. Silke TOBER, Berlin

Prof. Roberto M. UNGER, Law School, Harvard University, Cambridge, Ma.

Prof. Dr. Lev VORONKOV, International Institute for Peace, Vienna

Prof. Dr. Vitali ZHURKIN, Institute for European Research, Russian Academy of Sciences, Moscow

Drafting Commission:

Prof. Amit BHADURI

Prof. Jan KREGEL

Prof. Dr. Egon MATZNER

Dr. Leo SPECHT

Prof. Roberto M. UNGER

Sponsoring Institutions:

Austrian Academy of Sciences, Research Unit for Socio-Economics, Vienna

International Institute for Peace, Vienna

Science Centre Berlin for Social Research (WZB), Research Area Employment and Labour Market, Berlin

Vienna Academy for the Study of the Future

1. INTRODUCTION

The process of economic and social change initiated in 1989 brought expectations of better living standards to millions of Eastern Europeans. Over the last two years important steps have been taken towards the introduction of market-based economic relations. In 1992, the Republic of Russia and other successor States to the Soviet Union are prepared to follow their Western neighbours by eliminating price controls and by granting property rights for land to peasants. But citizens in these newly democratized countries have already started to question the ability of the market system to improve their material conditions and have started to become sceptical about the possibilities of changing their lot by their own individual efforts. Although the situation differs dramatically from country to country, and despite the partial signs of progress which appear to be emerging, the common citizen in these countries with the exception of the former German Democratic Republic, has suffered a substantial reduction in living standards: production is in sharp decline, the distribution of income is worsening, unemployment is increasing. These conditions are general to all countries. Today the vast majority of the population in these countries are living in economic conditions which are demonstrably worse than those experienced under the inefficiencies of central planning.

In 1990, the first year of transition, real wages in Poland fell by nearly a third and industrial output declined by 25 %. In 1991, output declined by another 19 %. While some of this decline was due to the fact that nonmarketable output is no longer included in calculations, the fall in production to date of over 50% far exceeds what can be attributed to a pair of shoes containing two left feet or the 100 pount nail of the anecdotes of the inefficiency of command systems.

In Czechoslovakia, where the transformation process started a year later, real wages fell by 25 %, with industrial output down by 21 % in 1991. Output was down by 26 % in the first quarter of 1992 compared to 1991, so the decline has been even more rapid than in Poland. And it is not yet finished; when privatization of state enterprises occurs this automn, the federal government will withdraw all subsidies, assuring additional losses in output and employment.

Even in Hungary, where a more gradual approach has been adopted, real wages fell by more than 5 % in 1990 and 1991 and industrial output fell by 19 % in 1991 and by 20 % in the first quarter of 1992 compared to 1991. Thus, in the three largest former command economies nearly half of pre-transformation industrial output has been lost since the beginning of the stabilization process.

No Eastern European country reported positive net investment for 1991 and the first estimates for 1992 suggest net investment outflows for 1992. Registered unemployment rose from under 2 % in 1990 for Hungary and Czechoslovakia to 8.9 % and nearly 9 % respectively in March 1992, while in Poland, the rise was from 6 % to over 12 %. In March 1992, there were nearly 2.25 % million unemployed Polish workers. The fall in real GDP for 1991 ranged from around 10 % for Poland and Hungary to 16 % for Czechoslovakia. In 1992, the figures are 1 %, 2 % and 7 % respectively.

There is, however, some indication that production conditions are starting to stabilize, and inflation rates have started to slow. In Hungary, inflation in the first quarter of 1992 relative to 1991 was 26 %, down from around 35 %, while in Czechoslovakia, it has fallen to around 20 % from above 50 %. In Poland, it has fallen to around 40 % from over twice that figure in 1991 and over 60 % in 1990.

The economies of the other recently democratized countries showed much sharper deterioration, while conditions in the Commonwealth of Independent States were generally less extreme, but are predicted to deteriorate rapidly. In Russia and the Ukraine, inflation is estimated to be around 1,000 % for the current year, but real output is expected to fall by only 13 %; real wages fell by an estimated 4 % in 1991 and by 35 % for the first quarter of 1992 with respect to the first quarter of 1991.

While some of these problems are unavoidable features of a radical transformation of a planned economy into a market economy, their severity and duration depends largely on the approach taken to transformation. In all of their various forms these programmes contain three basic measures:

(i) economic liberalization through the abolition of controls over prices and production;
(ii) macro-economic stabilization through control of the money supply and balancing of the government budget;
(iii) the sale of State property to private individuals/corporations.

Differences in the programmes of particular countries only concern the speed and method of implementation.

Thus, while there is no question that these three basic measures are necessary for the transformation process, there can be differences concerning the extent and timing of their application.

In particular this is the case with respect to the economic liberalization measures which comprise the elimination of price controls, the introduction of free external trade through the reduction and elimination of tariffs, quotas, and monopoly licensing of trading firms, and the introduction of legal regulation governing private property in the form of a commercial code, company law, and the judicial enforcement of contracts. It is the large number of incentives they provide for economic performance that is important for the transformation process.

Macro-economic stabilization has taken the form of reduction and/or elimination of price and production subsidies, devaluation of the exchange rate and currency convertibility, and restrictive monetary policies to reduce the growth of domestic credit sufficiently to produce positive real interest rates. Finally, the privatization of State enterprises, by transforming them into corporate forms capable of being sold or distributed by some other means to private sector owners, has become the cornerstone of each transformation programme. It is usually assumed that this in itself is sufficient to provide the incentive required for wealth seeking activity by economic agents, as well as to provide, in line with early liberal political thought, the polity of a property owning democracy.

By early 1992, it became clear that the measures so far undertaken have been combined in such a way that will not lead to the desired results. What is currently being proven by facts can also be explained in analytical terms. The central error which is common to all of the existing transformation programmes is to believe that the simple elimination of central planning and the introduction of private ownership of property will automatically generate the market system which is considered as the necessary and sufficient condition for wealth creation in the newly liberated nations. The idea that the market can be introduced simply by freeing prices and production from controls and by creating private ownership relies on fundamental misunderstanding of the operation of market capitalism. The market is not a deus ex machina, nor a mysterious force operating through an invisible hand. The market is a social institution which has been nurtured and developed over centuries by conscious human action. The market is a complex network of signalling devices, only one of which is represented by the prices determined by voluntary exchange by individuals of existing goods and services. Since the market deals with the current impact of past decisions and the anticipations of future conditions generated by current and past conditions, it is embedded in a socio-economic context of regulations and interpersonal relations and expectations. The successful introduction of the market mechanism can only take place in the context of the reconstruction of the socio-economic fabric of the former centrally planned economies.

In the mixed market economies of Western Europe, the social and economic contexts in which markets are embedded emerged by a combination of spontaneous action and public intervention. The economic and social conditions currently prevailing in Central and Eastern Europe do not permit the luxury of the waiting for spontaneous solutions; conscious public action has become unavoidable. AGENDA presents basic principles which should be seriously considered in the preparation and evaluation of a transformation programme aiming at the reconstruction of the socio-economic fabric of former communist countries based on decentralized initiatives coordinated through market forces. The notion of socio-economic context in itself precludes the idea of proposing a universally applicable transformation programme. Instead, programmes must be formulated by relying on local knowledge in each specific context. Therefore,

AGENDA should be considered as a document providing a set of guidelines, not as a specific blueprint.

The guidelines proposed as integral parts of a successful transformation programme are derived from an investigation of the emergence and operation of advanced market economies. They also rest on a recognition that we may learn from historical experience of both successful and catastrophic socio-economic changes.

One example of a catastrophic experience is represented by the developments of interwar Europe. Based on the principles of macro-economic stabilization similar to those currently being applied in Eastern Europe, and in the absence of international co-operation, the successor States to the Austro-Hungarian Empire did not achieve economic self-sufficiency and, as a consequence, lost their newly acquired political independence. A series of similar experiences can be found in the recent history of the Latin American countries which have failed to recover sustained economic growth in the wake of IMF-type stabilization policies.

On the other hand, examples of successful socio-economic reconstruction and development may be seen in the countries which survived and emerged from World War II as democratic market economies. The World War II reconstruction in Western Europe was clearly based on market forces. All the elements included in the three transformation measures cited above were not implemented at once, but gradually over a period of some 40 years. The process of reconstruction was based on a widespread system of controls and regulations which repressed inflation and wages and allowed control, in particular, of exchange and interest rates as well as of prices of basic goods, and the existence of public property. This system was dismantled slowly over decades in step with the expected capacity of market forces to solve the problems. Equally important in this process was foreign aid from the United States under the Marshall Plan and in various other forms. It relieved the initial scarcity of foreign exchange which was required to reconstruct and modernize infrastructures and productive capacity. It also required the recipients of aid to formulate a detailed economic recovery plan detailing the ways in which funds would be used. In addition the Marshall Plan also provided the funds necessary to establish the European Payments Union, a mechanism which made possible the multilateral settlement of trade balances within the area of the reconstructing countries without recourse to bilateral trade restrictions. The only trade restrictions were indirect, as imports required payment with scarce US dollars.

Reconstruction programmes designed on the principles of the transformation programmes currently being applied in Eastern Europe would almost certainly have prevented the economic miracles of post World War II Western Europe. The other, and even more spectacular success story, is Japan, and the Little Tigers (Hong Kong, Singapore, South Korea and Taiwan). Although all of these countries have based the increasing strength of their economies on market forces, they have never renounced to policy intervention in the name of a sacrosanct defence of the operation of market mechanisms. On the contrary, by 'governing the market' and learning from it in a pragmatic manner they have succeeded in creating socio-economic conditions which have stimulated the expansion of production capacities and increased competitiveness in a spectacular manner. Both the catastrophic and the successful historical examples emphasize the urgency of governing the forces of the market in Central and Eastern Europe by promoting the socio-economic reconstruction. The need for such an approach is even greater due to the complete rupture of the social and economic structure inherent in a rapid and unforeseen shift from a centrally planned to a market economy.

In addition, the international economic environment which the transforming countries have to face is currently much more complex and challenging than it was in the post-war period. In World War II most countries had experienced severe damage and dislocation to their economic and political structures, while today's transforming economies are directly confronted by trade rivals from technologically advanced economies, all of whom are facing conditions of substantial excess-production capacity. Further, in the 1940's and 50's the USA, the major surplus country, was confronted by the threat of a global communist take-over which the European Recovery Programme was designed to prevent; the former communist countries cannot yet count on the self-interested aid of the wealthy industrial nations.

In summary, there seems to be no way to justify the absence of active policies aimed at creating the appropriate socio-economic context necessary to allow the successful operation of the market mechanism in producing the transformation of the former command economies into free market democracies. AGENDA proposes a discussion of five main topics which must be seriously considered while designing appropriate active policy intervention in the frame of concrete transformation programmes. They are:

1. Making the Socio-Economic Context;
2. Creating the Market;
3. From Destruction to Production;
4. From Economic Emergency to Growth;
5. Making the International Context.

Throughout, the discussion will try to address explicitly the individuals - may they be persons, principals or agents - that are required to take action in order to achieve either directly or indirectly, the proposed outcomes. It is true that competitive markets can make men act. But in order to make markets produce acceptable outcomes, they have first to be created by men.

2. MAKING THE SOCIO-ECONOMIC CONTEXT

A socio-economic context is the everyday economic surrounding in which individuals act. This refers to the consumer, the worker, the clerk, the manager or all who are engaged in producing, distributing and consuming the national product of a society. As everyone knows, an individual's surroundings represent constraints which promote and prevent, reward and punish his or her actions. The transformation from a centrally planned economy to a market economy is equivalent to a complete change of the socio-economic context conditioning the behaviour of each citizen. A socio-economic context may be reduced to four basic elements:

(1) The world view underlying individual decisions and actions;

(2) the institutions (markets, laws, decrees, norms, habits etc.) which influence decisions and actions in a positive and/or a negative way;
(3) the reward which accrues to individual effort and is signalled in relative prices and incomes;
(4) political actions which attempt to influence (1) to (3).

Only if these elements are perceived by people as a social context rewarding their own actions, investment, employment and output-producing socio-economic reconstruction will result.

2.1. The World View

What is the most important element in the socio-economic reconstruction of a disintegrating society? Contrary to current belief, it is not the abstract idea of a free market with price flexibility. Rather, it is the expectation of a large and increasing number of individuals that the overall level of well-being can be improved by their own personal initiative to improve their own positions. To be credible, such expectations must be based on realistic assessments of resource requirements and availability. Expectations must be such that they can be reasonably satisfied in the not too distant future.

Unfortunately, all transformation programmes which have been initiated since 1989 try to evoke optimistic expectations without providing a firm foundation for their realization. The ideal economic environment envisaged by current transition programmes centres around the private entrepreneur seeking profits in competition with other entrepreneurs in an unrestrained market. The same applies to the world of the consumer and the worker. In pursuing their private interests, they also contribute to the best possible outcome. The best strategy therefore is to expose sellers and buyers as fast as possible to unrestrained competition. The main task of policy is thus to destroy the existing impediments to freedom of action in economic affairs. Nothing more is necessary to insure prosperity.

However, such a view misunderstands the history of capitalist market economies. It is based on an ideology of the market that misinterprets reality in the same way as the ideology of planning under communist rule. A realistic perception of the operation of a market economy must acknowledge the crucial role played by money and credit. But, contrary to the conventional view, the importance of these factors is to be found in the fact that money, credit and markets are basic social institutions which themselves need to be embedded in appropriate institutions and guided by an adequate fabric of policies to function in a socially acceptable way. Without such an institutional and political framework, money, credit and markets will fail to provide the support necessary to lead to a successful introduction of markets.

Present transformation programmes, in particular those inspired by international lending institutions, suffer from an additional shortcoming. Their primary focus is on abstract targets such as economic stabilization, balanced budgets, balanced current account, convertible currency, etc., irrespective of the consequences of their policies on output, investment, employment and private consumption. In these strategies, what should be considered as the goal of individual economic activity, viz. the provision of goods and services to the individual consumer, is conceived of solely as a means for satisfying abstract monetary targets. In a strategy for socio-economic reconstruction, private consumption levels and sectoral output levels in key areas (such as food, housing, export trades) should be established as targets and the market forces, as well as the monetary devices used as instruments in achieving them, should be specified. A concrete idea of what may be achieved by individual effort is in a way as important as the personal reward to be expected.

Socio-economic reconstruction has to take two steps: First, it has to establish concrete targets which are both ambitious and realistic and then to work out contexts in which producers and consumers act in markets, supported by appropriate institutions and policies, but guided by market signals (relative prices and incomes). Through the institutionally supported pursuit of their own interest they would be induced to contribute to the realization of the established targets in terms of employment, production of output. It should be stressed that targets have to be defined in a parsimonious way. They should not be 'omni-comprehensive'. Apart from basic infrastructures, economic and social necessities in the fields of communication, energy production, etc. or in foreign exchange earning industries, production and distribution should remain untargeted and left to the market.

2.2. Institutions

Institutions may be defined as social rules and patterns of behavior ensuing from them. They allow people to live together, work together and also to settle conflicts. Such regular patterns of behaviour enable and support individual decisions and actions; they often can also restrain individual initiative. The most important institutions are human and civil rights, the family, property, the State, the market as well as habits and other unwritten conventions. They often emerge spontaneously and through repeated social interaction, but in many cases they have to be made by conscious action. According to conventional wisdom which underlies IMF-type strategies, 'institutions' and their associated 'regulations' are often regarded as inimical to 'competition' and 'free markets'. But, in reality, the two must be combined for the successful operation of either. The 'market', for instance, (both as an ideal and as a real type) also should be perceived as an institution. To a significant extent, competition, too, is dependent on contextual factors, i.e. the societal 'capsule' within which competition takes place; even economic behaviour which appears to be based on price incentives is also embedded in a social fabric of custom, habit and regulation. Simple reference to any of the world's major financial markets shows the importance of both informal convention as well as formal regulation.

One of the reasons for institutions, habits and convention has been highlighted by Keynes. It is the crucial role which uncertainty exerts in a monetary production economy. This uncertainty can have both a creative effect (to strengthen competitiveness because rewards are high, but uncertain) as well as a destructive impact (to defend against uncertainty by holding back money rather than making investments with highly uncertain future returns).

Institutions may reduce uncertainty, for they tend to introduce a degree of regularity and predictability into individual and collective behaviour. If successful, they may stabilize the expectations on future outcomes, which facilitate individual decisions and actions, in particular with respect to investment.

A second economic reason for the emergence of institutions in modern economies concerns the way in which abundant information is transformed into usable knowledge. Habits or rules of thumb are examples of such institutions. They allow economizing on the collection and processing of information (or on 'transactions costs'). Action may then be based on what has been called 'thoughtless rationality'.

A third basic feature of market economies is their inherent tendency to provide an insufficient amount of public goods which are often crucial for successful economic performance: hence non-market institutions, for instance, are needed for the supply of education, training and research and development. We can therefore conclude that institutions are an inherent element in the operation of market economies. The specific way in which institutions matter, whether they assist or constrain initiatives, cannot, however, be deducted from theoretical considerations alone.

Whether institutions (or markets) effectively support or constrain economic performance and employment has to be evaluated also on the basis of empirical evidence. The transformation of a planned economy into a market economy cannot avoid decisions concerning public action. It is a trial and error process in which the government and the legislative bodies try to stimulate the private interest of those engaged in the production and distribution of output for the pursuit of socio-economic reconstruction.

2.3. Price and Income Signals

Price and income signals are indispensable in a market economy: they inform sellers about opportunities to increase their revenue and buyers about opportunities to save money. This information acts at the same time as an incentive to redirect sales and purchases. In a well-balanced economy there are few reasons for trying to influence relative prices and incomes. This is not the case in economies with large internal and external imbalances. In such a situation, which currently characterizes Central and East European economies, the radical liberalization of prices is likely to produce destructive rather than beneficial effects on economic reconstruction. This can be clearly seen in the effect of the liberalization of two key prices: (i) the exchange rate and (ii) the interest rate. All post-communist economies suffer from the absence of internationally competitive tradable goods, which produces substantial current account deficits. Sudden liberalization of the exchange rate would only lead to a sharp devaluation which increases the price of imported goods, making the maintenance and expansion of internal production capacities uneconomic. This in turn would simply intensify the imbalance between supply and demand.

In a similar way, in conditions of high risk and a savings shortage, the freeing of interest rates would result in a sharp increase in rates so as to be an obstacle to the expansion of capital investment. Similar considerations apply to the price of labour which in unionized industries could be driven above levels compatible with international competition and in non-unionized industries kept below levels sufficient to provide adequate demand for output. Therefore, the relative prices and incomes in areas which are crucial for socio-economic reconstruction should be liberalized only gradually and be subject to institutional devices as well as policy measures to keep them at levels which promote desired supply conditions without destroying demand. This is a difficult task with liberalization as the aim to be approximated in line with the reduction of imbalances.

In the broader macro-economic context, the creation of a level of effective demand sufficient for the amount of investment necessary for socio-economic reconstruction is an essential part of a policy aimed at producing the appropriate price and income signals. This might take the form of an incomes policy which tries to make the increase of wages compatible with the spur to labour productivity. It goes without saying, that the increase of wages should also correspond to the growth of output of consumption goods. It is a method of co-operation which, if successful, is rewarded by higher competitiveness, greater output and more jobs. This co-operation, if regularly repeated could become part of the institutional context of the economy, as is the case in a number of economies in Western Europe.

2.4. Public Action and the Role of the State

The emergence of a civil society and private action based on private interest is the very essence of the transformation of the system of central planning into a market economy. In this process the State as law-giver and enforcement agency has to play an important role. The role of the State cannot, as is often conceived in IMF-inspired transformation strategies, be a self-liquidating one which, in the end, restricts itself to the simple guarantee of law and order. The 'invisible hand' attributed to competitive markets is not sufficient to guide socio-economic reconstruction. The urgency of the task does not permit the time required for the emergence of spontaneous processes. Therefore, there is an urgent need for an active State which, by conscious policies, promotes the growth of production.

Adam Smith and the English classical liberal economists also accorded an active economic policy role to the State. In their view the 'invisible hand' is always guided by the legislator who is to design a legal framework which excludes possibilities of outcomes which are not compatible with public welfare. In the view of Lord Robbins, the classical economists were convinced that the pursuit of self-interest, unrestrained by suitable legislative constraint, carried no guarantee of anything except chaos. This attitude is the opposite of that which inspires presently existing transformation programmes. It implies that if market forces are not restrained, economic chaos and then political disorder will follow. By attempting to balance private interest and social welfare, the State plays a decisive role in any transformation strategy. Once more, it is important that the individuals serving the State share, out of their own interest and conviction, a world view which attributes an important role not only to competition but also to public actions. This is another aspect which IMF-type transformation strategies neglect, and is an oversight which AGENDA seeks to remedy. It is true that the State power which was an important pillar of the old system has been drastically weakened with the collapse of the communist rule. In places where it still is prevalent, it has lost its legitimacy and thus its authority. This severe handicap will have to be overcome by the transformation societies. The success of economic policy in a reconstruction period largely depends on the support it receives from the major social groups. This is a lesson which can also be learned from comparing the successful examples of reconstruction after World War II with the unsuccessful cases after World War I. Therefore, it is a genuine task of a post-communist State to organize social consensus which aims at broad social co-operation in the process of socio-economic construction. In doing so, both the State and the political parties comprising it would gradually gain legitimacy and political authority.

One important contribution to social consensus and co-operation consists in distributing the burden of transformation in a fair way. The role of the State in this respect would be to guarantee that the increase of production and productivity goes hand in hand with a minimum provision of social services for children, sick and old persons. Another important issue is unemployment, which is bound to remain high until the reconstruction and expansion of capacity starts to create competitive jobs. Unemployment is not only a social evil; it also amounts to a destruction of skills. This is the opposite of what is needed if reconstruction is to take place. Therefore the State and the local authorities should try to organize training programmes in transitory establishments. Although such a scheme, at first sight, appears to be a burden to society, no society can afford to leave citizens who are disabled or out of work without a minimum standard of living. It appears appropriate to offer such a minimum guarantee in exchange for skills needed in the transformation period.

By 1992, it has also become evident that the conventional transformation programmes not only cannot rule out poverty and misery, they cannot even prevent local and temporal famines, e. g. in parts of the former Soviet Union. An examination of the history of famines suggests that neither famine nor undernourishment has much to do with physical shortages of food. The problem is always to be found in the maldistribution of existing supplies. Even in periods of acute shortage, the problem cannot be resolved by free distribution. In such situations, schemes should be preferred in which aid is received by the unemployed only in exchange for money or participation in public works. The equivalent to aid from abroad should be used for programmes which promote socio-economic reconstruction. The outlook and the experience of a steady improvement of living conditions is the most important factor in fostering an incomes policy in which the trade unions and professional groups refrain from income claims that are incompatible with average increases in labour productivity. Another important condition of success is the outlook and experience that by conscious action unemployment is going to be reduced and that productive employment in internationally competitive firms is steadily increasing. Nothing is more frustrating than living in a world where there is great scarcity of commodities and an abundance of idle labour not being used for the production of the goods needed. The idea is to link production and welfare from the very beginning of the reconstruction programme by inspiring economic agents to pursue their individual interests.

2.5. The Conception of the State in the Transformation Process

Not only have transformation programmes been conditioned by existing economic conditions, they have been constrained by the tenor of the political discussion of transformation. Transformation is viewed as a transition between two antagonistic social systems: 'socialism', thought of as the starting point and the first stage of post-communism, and 'capitalism', a superior and dominant form of social system. This dualistic approach expresses itself in dichotomies such as plan versus market, state versus society, public versus private. Policies are always evaluated with respect to their position in this dualistic view of the world, e. g. as the domain of the market is extended, the role of the state diminishes, etc. Economic and political transformation is thus represented as a linear process from one, outmoded, communist social system and a command economy to Western style democracy and a market economy.

But, the economic reality of adjustment in the former communist states has not followed this linear adjustment path between two opposed states. As a result there has been a rapid deterioration in public authority in post communist societies, even when democratically constituted. This currently presents not only a threat to political stability, but to the pursuit of successful tranformation.

As has been shown above, most historical experiences of successful transformation processes have avoided the sharp political and economic dichotomies which inform current discussions in Eastern Europe and have proceeded pragmatically, evolving systems which best have met actual conditions of transformation.

AGENDA thus argues against the currently prevailing dualist approach and the ideological dichotomies that result from it. Advanced social theory developed in the West has shown them to be obsolete. The supposed dichotomies have been ignored by all successful economic and social policies in Western Europe and the US since the beginning of the century. Western societies have adopted the programmatic approach of ideological purity which is now dominating in Central and Eastern Europe only at the expense of destroying the social consensus upon which these societeies have been founded. The rigidity and lack of flexibility which is contained in these dichotomies is one of the most serious impediment to the eliminiation of the communist system in Europe, for, paradoxically, they seem to preserve the old dirigiste methods.

Any real process of transformation should be open ended; it should allow for a variety of views and programmes, of interests and needs to compete against each other, and by doing so, to give a positive contribution to the transformation process. This is a precondition for the action of institutions and economic policy as a positive force in support of transformation as put forward in this AGENDA. The notion of public authority should not be viewed as the equivalent of the 'State'. It should represent the authority to implement rules of public conduct understood as ability of the social and economic process to regulate itself. Such rules can be thought of as stemming from two groups of sources. They might be handed down by the democratically legitimated legislators and be implemented by regulary (administrative) means. They might, however, be generated by way of contractual arrangements by social formations and gain force by virtue of their content and general acceptance. Both kinds of rules are necessary for maintaining the tranformation process.

Regulatory schemes which respond to the needs of transformation in process have to be a response to evolving conditions. They will have to make use of a variety of different methods. Such regulation has to fulfill a twofold task. It has to establish rules which are able to transform themselves in the course of the transformation process and it has to allow for the broadest possible participation of social actors and an exchange of a broad variety of social interests. The regulatory approach envisioned in this AGENDA should be the framework and catalycist for social experimentation. Social experimentation must lead to pluralism of social organizations corresponding to competing interests. Indeed, such pluralism would amount to pluralism of transformation programmes. In this sense, public authority is understood to be the guarantor that all programmes and approaches are given consideration as the system evolves toward its new social form, which will not be a return to communism, but neither is it likely to be the western style democratic market system by inspiring individual interests.

3. CREATING THE MARKET

Although the formerly planned economies are now introducing market-oriented economic systems, it is also the case that none of them are starting from scratch. They all have existing industrial and financial systems which have already been partially transformed. It is in solving this problem of the existing structure of the economy that the form of transformation has dominated the question of the essence of transformation. For both political and economic reasons, the first step undertaken in the transformation process was often to prepare State enterprises for privatization. This process of changing ownership has generally occurred independently of any concern for the structure of management control of the enterprises or the environment in which they operate. In most cases the existing managers and party bureaucrats have remained in positions of power.

3.1. How to Privatize the Planning Function

One particularly damaging error in the process of preparation for the privatization of State production facilities regards what in the Soviet system was called 'Gossnab', the State committee for supplies, responsible for centralized direction of the distribution of inputs and outputs. Hence it was a crucial instrument in plan implementation providing for the interface between different production units and between the production sphere and the retail sales outlets. An individual factory is a physical production unit which can be separated from the State and given a corporate form which closely resembles a Western firm. With the addition of a balance sheet it becomes a State-owned 'firm' which becomes a candidate for sale to a private owner.

The Gossnab, representing part of the State productive structure responsible for planning the logistics of the provision of inputs to the factory, for directing its output to retail outlets and so forth, being a part of the command system which is to be abolished, clearly cannot be privatized, it must simply be abolished as redundant in a market system. Indeed, in a market system, it is the market, or more precisely the system of wholesale markets, or networks of sales contacts and relations of the sales offices of large firms, which serve as the interface between producers and suppliers and producers and retail outlets. But, unless this complex system of market relations arises instantly and spontaneously with the elimination of State property and State control, the unique act of the privatization of the individual productive units of the former State enterprises may sever plants from suppliers and customers, leading to difficulties in survival as long as the network of personal and market relations which should replace Gossnab still is lacking.

There is another, equivalently damaging menace to the survival of productive capacity, which became reality in East Germany: the distribution system was quickly replaced by the networks of West German firms who only distributed their own products, cutting East German productive units off from customers and suppliers, irrespective of the price and quality of their output. Since, in a market economy, enterprises are valued not on their physical productivity, but on their ability to generate future cash revenues, the failure to provide a replacement for the state distribution network quickly drove the prospective profitability, and thus the economic value of East German productive units, to zero. In such conditions privatization was no longer a question of determining a fair sales price for the State 'firms', but of virtually trying to give firms away. Piecemeal privatization of productive units, without the complex set of market relations which accompany a private enterprise market system, is bound to fail. This argues in favour of late, rather than early privatization. It clearly underlines the big importance of the government taking active responsibility for the creation of the market system, which in this case is not an economic abstraction, but the physical existence of the network of wholesale markets, or networks of salesmen and supply offices of large firms, which operates in every capitalist economy.

3.2. The Role of the Financial System

The conversion of the financial system reflects the same partial understanding of the role of institutions in the market mechanism. Since in the State planning system individual productive units had no need of financing their operations via the market, there was no active role in decision-making undertaken by the banking system; financial relations with the rest of the world were operated through State banks specializing in particular activities, such as financing foreign trade.

In a command system, in the absence of financial constraints or rationing of capital via interest rates or loan covenants, macro-economic stability is assured by limiting advances to enterprises to their variable costs of production, the most important of which is the wage bill. The price level of final goods is set (including turnover taxes) so that the receipts from the sale of current output just equal the funds disbursed to the public as incomes. Since there is no private real or financial property to be purchased, except for consumer durables (such as automobiles), and all public services are guaranteed, there is no need, and there should be no desire for net accumulation of money balances by households. Any difference between the wage costs plus other variable costs and the sales value of consumption goods should equal the wages and other costs required for the production of investment and public goods; if not it has to be covered by turnover taxes. Since these capital expenditures are financed through the government budget and should be equal to turnover taxes, there is no need for enterprises or the government to issue debt. All funds allocated to the enterprises by the State bank comes back in sales receipts so that in equilibrium there would be no outstanding money circulation. Money is simply the oil of the wheel of commerce, it has no inherent utility; thus it will not be held as an asset: it is neutral. Since there is no other property to be purchased, net savings should also be zero.

When this macro stability condition is not met, for example, if prices or turnover taxes are not increased relative to wages, when the proportion of investment or government services in output rises, or when households refuse to purchase the current output of consumption goods which are made available to them, this imbalance takes the form of the (undesired) accumulation of cash or deposits. The accumulation of unsold (undesired) inventories of goods held by the enterprises in excess of goverment expenditures or the additional investment is thus being 'financed' by the households. However, this financing is not via the purchase of liabilities of the enterprises or the government, for in the absence of bankruptcy any shortfall in enterprise payments is automatically made good by the creation of additional funds by the State bank. This is the source of the 'repressed inflation' that is identified after the liberalization of the command economies as the so-called 'monetary overhang' which has to be eliminated as part of the transition economic stabilization policy.

But, this 'overhang' also represents what in a market system would have been lending from the household sector to the State and the enterprises, either directly through the sale of bonds and shares or indirectly through the intermediation of the banking system. The value of the households' credits in a market system would thus have been directly linked to the value of the enterprises; the inventories of unsold goods were the collateral against the housholds' deposits. If the goods were unsaleable and without value, then the credits which they secured should also be zero to perserve macro-economic equilibrium. This could have been achieved in one of two ways: unleashing the repressed inflation to reduce the real value of the deposits or simply undertaking a currency reform in which all outstanding money balances in excess of a predetermined minimum representing transactions balances were converted into credits to the enterprises or blocked deposits.

However, despite the fact that some transformation programmes opted for inflation, the transformation of the financial system did not proceed in a market-based fashion. Since the banks already existed, the transition from a command to a market economy suggested that, like enterprises, they should also be transformed in a way which made them resemble Western financial institutions and rendered them suitable for privatization. To this end, financial systems were reformed to create a 'Central Bank' and a number of commercial banks with wide-ranging privileges out of the monolithic government controlled State bank. The major liabilities of the pre-reform financial system were the issue of note and public deposits, the major asset, foreign exchange reserves. The Central Bank was thus formed with foreign exchange reserves and currency as its assets and liabilities, respectively.

The commercial banks were created with deposits as liabilities and the funds (including the additional funding necessary to meet payments due to the build up of unsold inventories) as assets that had been advanced to enterprises to allow them to meet plan allocations converted into the equivalent of commercial and industrial loans that were allocated more or less randomly.

Of course, the newly created 'loans' of the commercial banks also appeared as liabilities on the balance sheets of the enterprises to be privatized, and now had to be serviced at market interest rates from the receipts of sales in increasingly competitive open markets at prices with rapidly disappearing subsidies. This was meant to introduce 'market discipline'. The collapse of the internal distribution systems in East Germany and the rapid disappearance of the CMEA market in Hungary brought declines in prospective sales which made servicing of these loans improbable. Thus, many enterprises were created which at their birth had negative net worth as a by-product of the reform of the financial system. At one and the same time, this transformation created a banking system which from the beginning had a high proportion of impaired loans on its books and was thus extremely unwilling to lend additional funds to the newly formed enterprises, or any others, whithout government guarantees. It is estimated that 75 % of the loans on the two largest newly created (1990) Czech commercial banks are non-performing, while in Hungary the figure is said to have reached 20 % for the three largest commercial banks which inherited the entire enterprise loans previously recorded on the books of the Central Bank.

Added to this were the difficulties of determining the ownership of the enterprises in the transition period (e. g. work in progress or inventories cannot be used as loan collateral unless they are the property of the firm and as the private property laws were slow in being introduced this could not be proven). Thus, the only linkage between the real and financial sector, between the enterprises to be privatized and the newly created banks, was inoperative from the start and created not only technically bankrupt enterprises, but also a crippled banking system. Banks were caught between Western-inspired central bankers seeking macro-stability by control of monetary creation sufficient to create positive real interest rates and the clear government priority of keeping the technically insolvent enterprises afloat until they could be privatized. Any increase in the banks' lending rates to meet the rising market rates would mean having to increase lending to allow the enterprises to meet the highter interest payments. Thus, balance-sheets were further weakened. So the banks had the choice of either shrinking net interest margins or increasing their provisions.

Both measures cannot make them attractive privatization candidates or effective monitors of the use of bank funds by firms.

In a sense this approach to the transformation of the financial system is based on a form of double counting in which the so-called monetary 'overhang' appears twice as liabilities on balance sheets. Recall that under the command system, whenever enterprise receipts fell short of plan payments and unsold goods built up because households were refusing to buy and were accumulating deposits, additional funds had to be extended to enterprises. When this system is transformed into a Western-style banking system, the funding for the unintended inventory accumulation is thus included with the normal financing for current production as the liability of the banks to the public in the form of deposits and as the liabilities of the enterprises to the banks. By setting up the system in this way, the burden of the devaluation of the prospective value of the enterprises is born by both the newly created banks as well as by the firms, but not by the public who are the de facto creditors. Either the public's undesired monetary holdings should have been exchanged for enterprise debt (bonds or shares) or both the debt and the deposits should have been written off by means of a currency reform. Instead, they were usually made directly convertible into foreign goods. By this strange transformation of the command economy financial system into a Western system, the transition of enterprises was made more onerous and a financially fragile financial system was created at a stroke; substantial transfers of government funds were required to keep it solvent. These funds were direct transfers to households and, in general, financed consumption expenditures on externally produced goods and thus did nothing to aid the reconstruction of domestic industry, thereby increasing the long-term financial support required.

These problems were further exacerbated in East Germany by the rapid unification and conversion of firms' debts to DM and the rapid opening of markets which meant that the market interest rates on debt had to be paid from sales made in competition with West German producers. Despite the fact that enterprises debts were converted at a lower (2:1) rate than deposits (an average of 1.8:1), most enterprises found it impossible to meet the new balance sheet constraints and the banking system was only saved by merger with the large German banks, by massive transfers to enterprises and by support from the "Treuhand". Indeed, the discussion over the conversion rate of East to West German Marks concentrated on this point, not on the potential inflationary impact of the conversion rate between Ost Mark and DM. It was the value of the debts which the enterprises had to acquire which was the crucial issue. The closer the conversion rate for deposits was to unity, the greater the impact of the double counting and the heavier the debt service burden on the enterprises and the greater the effective loan losses of the bank and thus the greater the fragility of the financial system. It was in this context that the 'Bundesbank' argued for a higher conversion rate, closer to the effective market rate which ranged from 3 to 5 Ost Mark per DM. This over-evaluation of the debts of enterprises also created increased difficulties in privatization, for the purchasers of enterprises were not only buying outdated capital equipment with meagre prospects for the growth of future earnings, they were also buying perfectly certain prospective DM interest payments at market rates on enterprises' debt denominated in DM.

This type of reform might be termed 'top-down' reform. It starts by identifying what is necessary for the formation of a 'central bank' similar to those found in the West and then proceeds to model the financial system to that requirement. Just as privatization must lead to the production of new private property in order to increase wealth, the financial system must be set up to aid the production of new financial assets corresponding to the new property. The privatization of the enterprise and the financial sector simply transformed existing physical assets of State enterprises into private assets and created the financial liabilities to represent them. As a matter of fact they already existed without representing any economic value in the terms of future production of real or financial assets. This is what might be called 'backward looking' privatization, and it cannot create a market mechanism because it creates no new economic value to be exchanged.

The appropriate approach to the financial system must then include both the process of 'liability destruction' and 'asset creation'. The process of liability destruction would involve the decision to destroy valueless liabilities which no longer are supported by economic assets in order not to burden the reconstruction period. This is what occurs in a monetary reform when only a small proportion of the outstanding currency, representing necessary transaction balances, is converted to the new issue. This was the procedure followed in the West German recovery. It was instrumental in setting the stage for strong balance sheets of German firms in the post-war period which enabled them to finance accumulation internally. Germany does not seem to have been put at a disadvantage because it did not move quickly to introduce widespread shareholdings and primary capital markets.

The creation of assets can only occur as a result of the successful production of a new wealth by means of financing via the banking system which also requires 'clean' balance sheets to function efficiently in initiating the transformation process. The perceived need to proceed by privatizing existing assets has thus jeopardized the possibility of both 'asset destruction' and 'asset creation' necessary for a successful transformation.

3.3. The Market Maker

The market is not an impersonal calculating machine predating the computer age. Nor is it the mythical 'invisible hand'. It is a social institution and thus the outcome of human actions. As such it can take different forms at different times and under different conditions. The 'market' is made up of a fabric of buyer-seller relations, not all of them resulting in actual transactions. None of those interpersonal relations and none of the resulting actual transactions can occur without agents who transmit information and function as middlemen. The middleman (intermediate) who establishes the link between the producer or seller and buyer (consumer, salesman or producer) is the market-maker. There can be no market economy without 'market-makers'. In a capitalist market economy distributors and wholesalers, with the aid of bankers, play this role. What does the market-maker do when he 'makes' the market? He may be an intermediary or he may take a more active role by placing orders for output at the producer before production takes place which he sells to buyers located at different places for delivery at later dates. When he places a firm order with a producer he creates collateral which may allow the banker to extend credit to the producer. This credit enables a producer to pay the wages to the workers, to buy the raw materials, energy services etc. from his suppliers. As the development of the division of labour reaches a higher level, special banks take the role of extending credits.

The function of the middleman as the market-maker is indispensable; but he does not appear like a deus ex machina. In order to exercise his functions the middleman needs a legal framework which enables him to conclude a variety of contracts and monitors and enforces their fulfilment. The law-giver is thus necessary for the making of the market as is the legal system which enforces contracts. And, last but not least, in cases where the market-maker takes position by buying before he sells or by acting as a distributor holding his own inventory he requires capital of his own or co-operation with the banking system to finance his positions. Before the full development of the banking system it will be the 'middlemen' who will be making loans to the producer and the retailer. In many cases he will function as both wholesaler and lender. In other cases, particularly as development advances and in industries producing investment goods, the role of the 'middleman' will become fully integrated in the sales and marketing division of the firm.

The actions of the market-maker in arranging transactions between the selling and buying agents are not without cost. These costs include collecting of information, the decision-making involving uncertainty, the stipulation and enforcement of contracts, etc. These costs will vary according to different forms of market organization. This is the message of Ronald Coase, winner of the 1991 Nobel Prize in Economics. Particular market forms can be understood as institutions which emerge and survive due to the fact that they are the most cost effective way of organizing economic activity. The making of the market is an entrepreneurial activity with a long history: This is another important message of the Nobel Laureate Ronald Coase. It is thus not sufficient to simply assume that 'the' market will emerge spontaneously. Thus, in the case of the former centrally planned economies, the question of the desired form of market organization and of the creation of conditions under which that market form can develop, must be actively debated and form part of the transition plan. It is a telling irony that the transformation programmes of the advocates of free markets appear to have forgotten Coase's important ideas that markets require individuals to make the prices and transactions that appear in them and that this is an economic, and thus costly, activity. It is not surprising then that in the concrete transformation programmes the actual problem of making the market was neglected. In the case of the former GDR it was left to the West German producers who quickly extended their distribution networks to East Germany, thereby excluding East German producers from their domestic markets.

4. FROM DESTRUCTION TO PRODUCTION

The improvement of the quantity and quality of goods and services available to consumers is the most important aim of a transformation programme. A programme which does not achieve this objective can be judged a failure. As noted above, the increase in quantity and improvements in quality of output cannot be achieved simply by abolishing central planning, liberalizing prices and privatizing State-owned companies because these actions do not provide any guarantee that a free market system will actually result from these actions. In the absence of formal action to provide for the development of markets and market-makers these actions may simply lead to a decline in production and in the general standard of living. This seems to be the result in most Eastern European economies today. The major priority in introducing the market system must thus be to stop and to reverse the current economic decline.

4.1. Emergency Programme for Production

The accumulated economic, social and political problems of the former centrally planned economies call for an immediate action programme. The transformation of these societies and economies must be recognized as a process through time in which the short-term measures are linked inextricably with the longer-term goals and policies. The immediate measures must act in accordance with the longer term goals, rather than contradicting them. A major problem with conventional stabilization policies, encouraged by the IMF and orthodox economic theory is that they place avoidable and unnecessary strains on the longer-run goals and objectives of the society in an attempt to solve the immediate economic problems of balance of payments, inflation, etc. It is painfully being recognized, e. g. in Poland and in Hungary, that market-oriented stabilization policies do not lead automatically to a process of sustained growth. Even more important is the recognition that stabilization, especially 'shock therapy', may impose social costs which are so great as to become politically unacceptable or unsustainable. There is a danger of the initial political goodwill and popular support for economic change being rapidly dissipated, destroying social cohesion and spreading disillusionment with the revolutions that had begun in the former centrally planned economies.

On the economic front, the central organizing principle around which the emergency programme needs to be conceived is the maintenance of production in conditions which respect the historical and structural characteristics of the individual economies. A main criterion is to minimize the loss of useful production during the emergency programme. Production which is not perceived to be useful for the civil society, e. g. a substantial part of military production or bureaucratic and secret police surveillance, should be eliminated. Although the production of such goods and services is not useful under new conditions, their disappearance and the resulting fall in employment would typically create a problem of deficient demand and lack of aggregate purchasing power in the economy. For an intelligent management of aggregate demand, a compensating increase in public investment may be needed, especially in areas of physical and social infrastructure, such as housing, health and education which have relatively little direct import content. They would have the double advantage of not over-straining the balance of payments and at the same time create greater consensus and popular support for the new economic emergency programme.

It has become almost fashionable to argue that the quality and the range of products in the formerly centrally planned economies are so poor that their destruction is first needed before a new, better and internationally competitive production can be created - a Schumpeterian process of 'creative destruction' of capitalism is what is required. This is an error of over-simplification for two reasons. First, 'creative destruction' presupposes the existence of a class of capitalist entrepreneurs eager to take up the opportunities for new investment. When, for historical reasons, this class does not exist, 'destruction' may simply remain 'destruction', without leading to 'new creation' as is becoming painfully obvious in many countries. The error is to believe that destruction creates automatically the new class of entrepreneurs; it does not, and may even thwart the emergence of the new entrepreneurial class because of the general economic disarray. Indeed, instead of creating an entrepreneurial class, such an economic climate may encourage various forms of black-marketeering, unfair trade and rent-seeking, i.e., encouragement of short-term speculation rather than entrepreneurship. Second, many of these poor quality goods are worth eliminating through a liberal import policy, provided the country can maintain this import capacity through export sales and inflow of capital on a sustained basis over time. Again, it is becoming painfully apparent that in most instances, such an adequate level of import capacity is not sustainable over time. The result is the worst of both worlds - the poorer quality consumer goods disappear without being replaced by permanent supplies of better quality goods. To maintain the standard of living of the majority, it is therefore necessary to carefully phase out the poorer quality goods through a selective and sustainable import policy. The essence of this policy is the time-phasing: enterprises producing poorer, unacceptable quality products must be given deadlines well in advance, e. g. two to four years and, also given some tactical support during this period in terms of free imports of essential raw materials, intermediate inputs, credit policy, technology transfer, and so on, strictly on the understanding that they will have an inflexibly limited period to restructure, to improve the quality of output and to reduce costs.

In this context, it is also essential that workers whose jobs and livelihood are at stake in these enterprises must be given some say in assessing the performance of the management and in contributing to a more effective restructuring at the micro level of the enterprises. Similarly, management must have total control of hiring and firing. One of the most important economic advantages of this strategy is that not only does it allow or at least give these enterprises a fair chance to survive by adjusting over time to the new conditions, but even more importantly, the drop in the domestic level of supply of poorer quality products becomes phased out and gradual, reducing the burden of sudden adjustment. This is also an essential ingredient of industrial policy in the short run, which would strengthen rather than weaken the longer run objective of industrial restructuring. In many instances, it may be less costly and easier to adapt and rationalize existing enterprises than to destroy them through an indiscriminate, but unsustainable liberal import policy in the name of market discipline.

To sum up, the main thrust of the emergency economic programme should be to create the minimum possible disruption to civilian supply in the short run. Since this will run parallel to conversion of the military sector and reduction of the military expenditure, intelligent demand management would require a flexible attitude to government expenditure. Thus, the compensation of higher public expenditure in physical and human infrastructure through less restrictive credit and more accommodative monetary and fiscal policies should be accepted as a possible component of the emergency programme, in contrast to the austerity measures of tighter credit and 'sound public finance' policies encouraged invariably in

IMF-style stabilization programmes. Minimum disruption of useful civilian production is the needed strategy in the short run for two interrelated reasons. It minimizes the social cost associated with unemployment, while it also directs the objective of public expenditure more towards production than toward simply creating a safety net for retrenched workers. A peculiar shortcoming of the orthodox stabilization strategy is that it first inflicts massive social cost in terms of the dislocation of production and unemployment and then discusses the safety net. Instead, the resources required for the safety net should be economized by minimizing intelligently the fall in production in a phased manner over time and in line with a reconstruction of production.

One aspect of the 'backward-looking' and 'top down' strategy has proved to be particularly damaging to the preservation of useful production: the decision to place all trade on a hard currency basis and to move as rapidly as possible to full exchange convertibility, again mimicking the form but missing the essence of a market system. The move to hard currency dollar and DM trade meant that hard currency had to be earned and held in reserves, and thereby simply granted additional seignorage rights to Germany and the US. This is the equivalent of lending to these developed countries. In conditions in which capital is scarce, this is not a sensible policy. Second, it means that intra-East European trade is restricted to these countries' export earnings with convertible currency countries, which is a constraint without economic rationale. Since the CMEA countries were integrated production and trading units (much as the Austro-Hungarian Empire) the move to hard currency trade is much like the break-up of the Empire, producing shortages of essential inputs, raw materials and replacement and spare parts which brought production to a halt and substantially lowered levels of income. While there is no reason to believe that these same trading patterns will be maintained after transformation has been achieved, there is no reason for them not to be preserved during the period in which the main preoccupation is to maintain incomes stable at or above subsistence. In most cases, the move to hard currency trade has produced an increase in bilateral and barter relations between countries, moving them farther rather than closer to the goal of multilateral free market exchange.

The great merit of an emergency programme which does not make a virtue of mindless austerity is its impact on the socio-political context. Greater flexibility with respect to government expenditure and credit policy to support programmes for social investment is the most powerful instrument we have for building popular support during the most difficult period of economic transition. Economic austerity is not a virtue in itself, and it is both bad economics and unacceptable politics to sharpen social conflict in the name of austerity rather than build up social co-operation and popular support through a less dogmatic set of policies.

4.2. Contracts as Forms of Property and of Control

In the market system profit is earned as an incentive to encourage the seeking out and satisfactory completion of future performance contracts, it is not earned as the result of the mere ownership of property. It is for this reason that the mere sale of State assets cannot ensure the transformation of the former command economies. This is especially true of large enterprises which are transformed into public ownership, leaving managers in charge who are often the same managers who operated under State ownership and who are now not even responsible to party officials or plan targets. At the same time, it is difficult to create owner-manager responsibility when no single individual has sufficient personal capital to acquire controlling ownership without the help of outside finance from the banking system. In conditions in which no potential manager can show past performance efficiency, banks have no way of judging who should and should not be given control of enterprises and there is a distinct risk that positions of control will be allocated in just as arbitrary a way as it was under State planning. The problem of joining control and responsibility to financial return is one of the most difficult problems to be faced in ensuring transformation. It is clear that there will be great temptations for managers operating companies awaiting privatization, or which are privatized but have little prospect of surviving in a competitive climate, to arrange for the sale of assets to create present remuneration, or simple 'asset stripping'. One possibility would be to adopt the market system procedure of managers' contracts based on future performance and profiteering. Managers could be hired on a low, fixed salary basis, with minimum performance targets in terms of profitability, market share and so forth to ensure that the targets are not met by asset stripping. Performance in excess of these targets would be paid in terms of bonuses formulated in terms of options on shares in the company. Thus a manager could start with say a 5 % or 10% stake in a public company and any performance above the target would be compensated with additional shares or with cash payments and options to buy shares at the price prevailing when he took over operation. A successful manager, who takes responsibility and exercises it, will be rewarded with eventual control of the company which he has earned by his own operation of the company. The operation of this type of plan would require that a controlling percentage of the shares of any existing enterprise be held by the government or a State holding which must be formally restricted by interfering with the operation of the management except to monitor contract performance.

Throughout this discussion, the emphasis has been placed on the fact that capitalism is a forward-looking process, based on the stipulation of undertakings which, on a contractual basis, will usually take place over a period of time. These stipulations of future performance represent exchanges which are subject to specification by contract. It thus requires contracts which regulate the ownership of physical property, of the type specifying the ownership of physical assets such as land, it also requires contracts which regulate actions in terms of performance. The difference may be seen for example in terms of a property contract which gives the individual the ownership of a physical piece of capital equipment and a contract which gives the individual ownership of the collection of contracts to pay labour, to sell products and so forth. The current specification of a contract governing share ownership is of the latter type, for it gives the owner the right to the flow of income from the collection of rights and obligations contracted by the firm. The process of creating the market through the creation of new private property will require a legal system which is centered not on physical property contracts, but on future performance contracts and will require specific methods of monitoring compliance. It is from this contract law that the control of the market must descend, in the form of anti-trust law, regulation of unfair trading and so forth. When satisfying a future performance contract leads to someone else not satisfying his own contract, a conflict arises which may represent the normal free market competitive process or may simply represent market manipulation.

A proper understanding of the questions at issue turns on the distinction between property and contracts. Although this distinction has been subject to criticism and has now been superseded by advanced Western jurisprudence, it is useful in pointing out an aspect that is absent in the privatization proposals in currently implemented transformation programmes in Central and Eastern Europe: the relationship between the privatization of property and the privatization of entitlements to obtain wealth.

Entitlements to participate in the social process of wealth formation derives from rights over property. In this respect, socialism was faithful to the tradition of

European liberalism, and the transforming countries are continuing in this tradition. It is thus of greatest importance to understand the structure of ownership and property rights now being created in these countries and to reflect on the social order that may be expected to emerge from these structures.

Current reforms focus on the creation of private property rights as distinct from state control of property. This privatization of property suggests a regulatory potential which is exploited in all Western countries. But, as the decision to introduce private property is based on the presumed ideological superiority of private over state control of property, any regulation of property by the state in the process of transformation has been rejected as contradictory. This position is based on a reduction of the idea of peoperty rights to the exclusive power and privileged dominion of the individual over things, so that any state interference with these rights is viewed as a return to state control of property. Western jurisprudence has avoided this conclusion by means of diverse understanding of property rights which was a major element in support of the regulatory changes which were instrumental in overcoming the great depression.

Such a diversified interpretation of property, which represents the jurisprudential foundation for the introduction of regulation in the process of transformation based on privatization, is absent in today's Eastern European discussion. This fact provides a valuable insight into the failure of traditional strategies of privatization in Central and Eastern Europe, where privatization is currently understood to be the process of a change from public to private control. Particular assets are made available to control by individuals. Privatization is reduced to the process of establishing private entitlement to 'own and use' productive assets.

This simple understanding of property as the power to 'possess, use, and dispose of things' has been abandoned by advanced Western jurisprudence which has instead proceeded on the basis of property as a 'bundle of rights'. Accordingly, not only the distinction between property and contracts, but, most importantly, the distinction between public and private retains only relative importance. Two basic sources of regulatory mechanisms have been mentioned above. By viewing property as a bundle of rights, the two merge into one. Property as a bundle of rights sets the framework for the tranformation process, set out in this AGENDA, and provides a jurisprudence for this approach as well as suggesting the possibility of new appraoches to the problem of the distribution of social wealth.

5. FROM EMERGENCY TO ECONOMIC GROWTH

While the priority of any revision of the current transformation from a centrally planned economy to a market economy must be to stop the current decline in output, there is general agreement that the next steps must be to remove serious internal and external imbalances and then to launch a process of sustained growth. At the core of the problems of imbalances is, most visibly, the shortage of a quantitatively and qualitatively adequate supply of marketable goods on the one hand and an enormous accrual of money on the other hand. Money is printed in increasing amount to pay the salaries of public sector employees, to fund transfers to the old and sick as well as for subsidies to firms making losses for paying wages. The task to be solved by a transformation strategy for socio-economic reconstruction is to stimulate the production of an internationally competitive output and at the same time to reduce excess demand. The transformation programmes which so far are in practice or are planned, place the reduction in demand at the top of the list of measures to be taken. This first step is taken in the expectation that investment and growth of output will follow as a result of the spontaneous operation of the forces of the market. It will be shown below that such a logic does not exist. In a transformation strategy which focuses on stimulating production and growth, a stable price level is necessary to discourage commodity speculation and to promote production on the basis of calculable relations between sellers and buyers. A uniform reduction of the money supply plus an increase in interest rates may bring about a break in inflation, although it is not at all certain to what extent and how long. It is, however, certain that, by the destruction of effective demand, this strategy is bound to reduce production and to discourage investment with adverse effects on macro-economic stabilization in the medium term as a consequence.

5.1. Monetary and Fiscal Policy

Existing transformation proposals place great emphasis on macro-economic stability as a prior condition for transformation. Macro-economic stability, in the sense of controlling demand to accord with potential supply, is thus the quantitative aspect of the problem of controlling hyperinflation which is encountered on the price side by trade liberalization and exchange rate convertibility. While trade liberalization is generally a simple matter of eliminating subsidies and controls and convertibility only requires a decision on the extent of the necessary devaluation and the commitment of sufficient foreign credits to insure adequate foreign exchange reserves to enforce it in the market, the operation of monetary and fiscal restraint to control demand pressures presumes the operation of monetary and fiscal institutions which often do not exist or have to be introduced as part of the transformation programme.

In current conditions, with the exception of Hungary, there is no tradition of government revenue generation which can be manipulated to the ends of fiscal policy. The entire burden of fiscal restraint thus falls on expenditure reduction at precisely the moment when transfer expenditures can be expected to rise and when public investment in social infrastructure such as transportation and telecommunications will be an absolute prerequisite to the process of providing internationally competitive conditions of production. Since the latter can be foregone much more easily than the former, the structure of spending will tend to become biased, as it already is in numerous Western countries, in favour of income transfers at the expense of the capital expenditures necessary to attract investment and employment creation. In this way macro-economic stabilization becomes an impediment, rather than a prerequisite, for economic growth and reconstruction.

The idea that monetary restraint should be part of macro-economic stabilization tends to reinforce the tendency to try to operate solely on capital expenditures, for in the absence of a well-developed system of commercial bank lending to households and firms, monetary restraint cannot act directly on private sector expenditures by reducing lending. It can only work at the level of the central bank refusing to fund government expenditure. In this sense, although the contribution of monetary restraint to macro-economic stabilization is often represented as requiring positive real interest rates imposed by means of restrictions on domestic credit expansion, it is in reality simply another way of expressing the necessity for fiscal restraint. As to the financial system, it is not yet sufficiently well developed for interest rates to have an impact on expenditure nor is it possible to speak of lending to households and firms as significant components of domestic credit. In addition, the high interest rates further restrict the possibility of developing a financial system, by encouraging firms to move to internal financing which produces a profits inflation, and to increase inter-firm credits which means the development of an endogenous financial system outside the control of the monetary authorities. Thus, an active contribution of monetary and fiscal policy to stabilization policy requires the introduction of a full system of taxation on the one hand and a functioning commercial banking system on the other.

Although it is generally recognized that both the organization of the fiscal and financial systems will have a direct impact on economic structure and performance, the freedom of choice in this respect is probably rather limited. While it would seem rational to try to design a fiscal and financial system which supports the imperative of the generation of a market system of property relations and the generation of additional property in the form of national wealth, the implicit decision which has been taken by most Eastern European countries to seek admission to the European Economic Community or at least the European Economic Area, implies that their fiscal and financial systems will have to conform to EEC standards. For taxation this implies in particular some combination of value added and income taxation. If this is so, it is not the structure of the fiscal system, but the level of taxation which is variable during the transition. It would appear that there is more freedom in the choice of financial structure, but the current EEC approach of single licensing and home country control suggest that the German system permitting universal banking will become the dominant form of banking organization.

A stabilization programme which is aiming at socio-economic reconstruction measures of stabilization also has to include provisions for the financing of the production and investment processes. The production process in autonomous firms has to be based on internal capital as well as external capital in the form of credits. A first and logical step in creating the capital basis for modernization and expansion is to relieve the firms of the old debts stemming from the period of central planning. They are merely accounting items; if firms are required to repay them it would only have negative effects on the restructuring. In a second step, firms not taken over by private investors should be provided with internal capital. A way to do so would be the allocation of liquid funds by a public investment fund in exchange of shares in the firm's assets. In a third step external capital in the form of credits should be made available. One way to do this would be, as suggested above, to provide the means of payment for the production and circulation of final goods. For example, a producer holding a firm order from a wholesaler could use the contract as collateral for a loan from a trade and development bank. On completion and delivery of the goods the producer could draw a trade bill on the wholesaler and discount it eliminating his debts to the bank, which is now lending to the wholesaler against the finished goods. When the goods are sold to the retailer, the bill is repaid with the retailer's acceptance clearing the wholesaler's account with the bank which is now lending to the retailer against his inventory. On final sale the retailer repays the bank with the money originally lent to the producer to pay his production costs, in particular wages. The first step in setting up the financial system must then be thc creation of trade and development banks which will provide finance for the production, distribution and final sale of goods to the public. The most efficient method of arranging this circuit would be for the trade and development banks to offer legal tender transactions accounts to the public. In this way the trade and development banks become a clearing house in which the loans to producers are paid as wages to households who take them as bank credits. To the extent that households prefer to use part of their wages in legal tender, the trade and development banks must be able to discount bills with the monetary authority. Since the trade and development banks are simply providing transaction accounts for different levels of the production structure, there is no reason why they should not be a branch of the monetary authority. The net expansion of legal tender will then depend on the rate of expansion of production. This would provide a system with a purely endogenous means of payment, or better, a perfectly elastic supply of the means of payment. To some this will seem an invitation to inflation, but the system simply reflects the so called 'real bills' doctrine, representing lending against work in progess, or goods in inventory. Yet, some constraint on lending will be required, for lending against 'real bills' does not mean that they can be sold for real money. Here the traditional role of the banker in evaluating pro forma proposals retains its importance. The basic constraint on lending is the potential loss to the bank.

If the transition to a decentralized market economy is going to work, it can only do so if a financial system is created which is able to provide the means of payment for the production and circulation of final goods in the system. In particular, credit is necessary for financing the production and investment process as well as the wholesale distribution process. Macro-economic stabilization, which in the conventional transformation programmes focuses on eliminating excess demand only, has to allow also for the creation and expansion of the institutions and contract networks which finance the production and expansion of output as well as its distribution in a decentralized system. This certainly excludes the introduction of a monetary crash programme as implemented in Poland. In order to stimulate production and investment the reduction of excess demand should allow for a mildly expansionary level of effective demand. As this invites price increases, and may as well set a wage-price spiral into motion, a certain number of basic prices may have to be controlled in the medium run. They include, in particular, the prices of necessities for the private households as well as for the production economy, such as wages, energy, credit and foreign exchange. The liberalization of these prices should be planned to take place in line with the reduction of existing imbalances. Macroeconomic stabilization is not an end in itself. It derives its significance by laying the foundation for the necessary restructuring of the production and distribution system, and by a subsequent increase in investment, employment, output and real income. A successful closing of the gap between demand and supply is only possible if due consideration is given to the simple fact that the measures on the demand side become effective quickly, while the restructuring and expansion of output takes much longer. A shock therapy can only rely on the demand side; it thereby neglects the supply side. Its consequence is a decrease in output which in turn sets into motion a kind of negative spiral, leading to a further reduction of output. This is a context which is detrimental to private investment. Stabilization which does not promote output and investment paves thus the way for its own failure.

5.2. Industrial Policy

One of the major decisions of the transformation period is certainly related to the question what to produce for export and what to produce to substitute imports. This, again, cannot be left to the 'autonomous' market forces. It has been clearly demonstrated by Japan and the 'Little Tigers' that governing the market is a way to success which can be supported by 'triangular trade'. It was also demonstrated by the success of West Germany that a high degree of regulation - particularly in qualification policies and labour protection - need not be a hindrance but a comparative advantage on the road toward international competitiveness. There is no 'King´s Road' to achieving international competitiveness both in exports and import substitution. Competition by definition is never without risk. It is, however, quite certain that 'latecomers' in competition need institutional support, by national and international regulation, in order not to succumb to the already 'leading competitors'. It is impossible without access to 'local knowledge' to formulate concrete criteria for the promotion of exports as well as import substitution. It is, however, possible to make some comments on the use of industrial policy to reinforce the transformation process in selected areas. The most important sectoral tasks are the development of infrastructure, restructuring the energy sector, development of a production-enhancing service sector, reduction in material, energy and environment-using sectors.

The functional tasks are: decentralization of monopolies, productivity enhancement, creation of a network of small and medium enterprises (SME's) in co-operation with existing medium and large enterprises, establishment of forward and backward linkages between firms, attraction of domestic and foreign co-operation partners, (re)training of workers in all areas for modern skill requirements (managers, skilled workers, technicians, servicing and marketing personnel, etc.), specification of management tasks and environmental restructuring. Specific attention needs to be paid to the motivation and work organizations and working conditions. These tasks require an effective institutional setup.

At the national level a very broad Restructuring Programme must outline the major direction in which capital should flow and the desired framework for industry (e. g. sectoral composition of output, degree of competition, foreign and domestic capital). The instruments to achieve this are:

- Establishment of a sectoral priority ranking by means of the following indicators: high income elasticity of demand; rapid productivity enhancement potential (reflecting comparative advantage); siting and environmental consideration; quality of work;
- Such a ranking must be based on a survey of existing service and production facilities and an assessment of national (regional) strengths (advantages). The information inputs should come from Regional Development Associations which furnish information on the basis of a complete survey of the production capabilities of enterprises in the specific region.

  The Restructuring Programme would form the basis for:

  - Decisions on which existing enterprises should be decentralized (broken up), which parts developed and which closed down. These decisions need to be built up on the idea of establishing a long-term viable industrial system which is strongly interlinked (forward and backward linkages), as well as technical and economic co-operation.
  - Decisions on where new enterprises (or activities) are required; such decisions must contain ideas on how to attract foreign capital and technology (as

well as management know-how), as well as on mobilizing domestic capital and owner/managers.

- Projections of manpower requirements and, for the establishment of training centres and retraining facilities. These should be conducted within the present educational system, in close co-operation with existing enterprises.

- The Programme should review existing privatization policies and set incentives in order to effect changes on a priority basis. From an economic viewpoint, nothing precludes the State owning productive assets after the transition to the market system has taken place. They should not be those assets left over after private individuals or groups (foreign and domestic) have had their pick, but rather constitute industrial complexes (clusters) which are interlinked. In this review of the existing privatization policies it should be made clear that the transfer of ownership should take second place to the problems involved in the restructuring and decentralization of production facilities.

- If existing industrial production is to be viable in the medium run, it will initially require a certain degree of protection from outside competition, but exposure to increasing degrees of domestic competition. For this reason, trade liberalization should not be introduced at a stroke, but step by step.

- Decentralization will show the pressing need for management talent. It is proposed to attempt to attract retired Western managers to the reform countries for periods of up to one year, in order to conduct on-the-job training for domestic managers and potential owner-managers.
- Financial flows need to be directed towards the priority production areas by means of subsidies and selective credit policies. The latter must have definite limits and should not eliminate incentives for efficient production by providing capital cost-free to enterprise. They have to take account of the present conditions of severe capital shortage. Instruments, such as deferred interest and capital repayments, and other temporary measures should best be able to combine present needs with efficiency.
- The establishment of new enterprises in the priority production and service areas needs assistance. Barriers to entry must be broken down, know-how and financial assistance be provided. A system could be considered which encourages skilled workers to establish their own supply business around the existant medium and large enterprises. The

Programme for Restructuring should be reviewed once a year, but should have a long-run (strategic) time horizon.

5.3. Regional Policy

The present attempts to break up the large industrial combines typically takes the form of an abrupt separation of the individual plants and a radical down-scaling or shut-down of those departments whose future returns can hardly be calculated but which are crucial for long-term adaptability, such as the R&D and training facilities. At least two 'indigenous' innovation potentials of the old production systems should be institutionally protected from a counter-productive short-term economism.

(1) The chronic shortages of intermediate goods and the low reliability of suppliers, the central theme in the last 40 years of the Central and Eastern European economies, resulted in the formation of large maintenance and internal machine building departments (the 'Rationalisierungsmittelbau' in GDR jargon). Since these departments had to shoulder the main burden in ensuring a certain level of continuity of production, they enjoyed a rather privileged

position with respect to the allocation of investments. Hence, they were equipped with comparatively modern technology but also employed well-trained workers with an extraordinary level of craft skills and the ability to improvise. These essential sources for innovation and improvization located within the maintenance and machine-building departments are now, in many cases, shut down or forced into economic independence in order to radically cut down all resources and capacities that are not directly involved in the production process. However, as economically independent units, these departments will hardly survive. On the one hand, they lack basic managerial know how; on the other hand, they suffer from a lack of linkages with other (customer) firms, financing and supporting institutions.

(2) In the course of the decentralization of the combines, one of the most criticized features of the East European production model, the breath-taking ratio of in-house production, reveals some unexpected virtues. To be sure, these virtues do not refer to the ability to manufacture all the parts of a product. Rather, they refer to the necessity to deal with the integration of various, sometimes incompatible, technical subsystems within a single product. Thus, the large combines were forced to accumulate some

> sort of systemic know-how spanning the entire value chain, from the raw material to the final product. This creates the possibility of providing integrated and customized system solutions. However, this systemic know-how can only be turned to competitive advantage if some of the pre-existing interdepartmental linkages continue to exist. In any case, the truncated production plants that result from the current attempts to break up the combines will hardly be able to develop and to offer customized system solutions. In order to prevent an irreversible loss of these 'indigenous' innovation potentials, the rationalization of the combines must not simply focus on the micro-economic efficiency of the production process.

It is not the reduction of the manufacturing costs of products, for which there are no longer markets, that is at the top of the agenda but the development of competitive products. The conclusions are twofold. First, the policy of privatization and break-up of the combines must allow for 'redundant capacities', such as the technical and human resources for innovation, located in the maintenance and internal building departments. Although the future returns of these resources cannot easily be calculated, they are essential for long-term survival. Second, these redundant capacities cannot be provided by an individual firm. Rather, they should be provided by 'loosely coupled' networks that combine the complementary strengths of individual firms. Loose coupling allows for a sharing of the costs and risks involved with innovative projects without 'locking' firms into co-operative relations with partners whose future is highly insecure. Moreover, a loose coupling of firms allows them to benefit from the systemic know-how accumulated within the large combines. This approach, however, would imply to shift the focus of the current policy from the narrow perspective of increasing efficiency at the level of individual firms to the creation of 'enabling conditions' on the level of sectoral or regional production clusters. However, the fact that loosely coupled networks appear to be an efficient and adaptable institutional solution, does not mean that they will be created 'automatically' by market forces. Rather, success stories of such networks - on the regional (e. g. the 'Third Italy') as well as on the national level (Japan) - point to the central role of public institutions in initiating and stabilizing co-operative production networks. In Central and Eastern Europe, the development of networks seems even more dependent on the activities of Regional Development Agencies (RDA). First, RDAs, composed of the local firms' management, work councils, local politicians, consumer and environmental groups, appear to be necessary to uncover complements and hence, a potential for co-operation in the regional industrial base. A lack of awareness of complements, namely the resources and abilities of other regional firms, is a serious obstacle to co-operation. Especially the information of the smaller firms hardly goes beyond the knowledge of the assets of those combines to which they belonged. Traditionally, information was gathered and circulated along sectoral lines. However, regional networking calls for a cross-sectoral information base.

Second, the stability of well-known successful networks in the 'Third Italy' or in Japan mainly results from long lasting trust-based co-operative relations. However, State socialism prohibited not only the spread of the market in the past, but it also virtually eliminated any institutions of (local) civil society that might form the basis for such trust-based co-operative relations in the near future. To be sure, this lack of trust can also not be compensated by an RDA. However, in coordinating and mediating the relations within networks, RDAs could support relations until the mutual adjustments of the co-operating partners ensure the stability of relations due to the high costs of breaking off co-operation.

Since an interventionist policy that mainly focuses on the 'indigenous' innovation potentials (still) seems taboo, as it immediately would be suspected of trying to restore those paternalistic attitudes towards the State whose elimination is at the top of the reform agenda, the Central and Eastern European countries are putting great hope in the investment projects of large Western corporations. The large Western corporations are not only expected to transfer capital and the most advanced technical and organizational know-how to Eastern countries, but also to reshape the sectoral and spatial structure of their dilapidated economies. Such long-term structural impacts, however, seem to be added to five basic conditions.

(1) Regional linkages, particularly backward linkages with suppliers of components are the most important channel through which technological and organizational change is transmitted. Without business linkages that favour some sort of transfer or demonstration effects, regional firms will hardly be stimulated or supported by the plants of Western corporations in raising their technological level and in improving their organization. Moreover, without such linkages, regional firms are in danger of losing even more of their already modest technical abilities. Many of them are 'locked into' the clan-like relations with their ministerial contractors and traditional customers in Central and Eastern Europe, especially in the Soviet Union. Since these customers typically

order rather traditional, technologically less advanced products (e. g. machine tools without electronic control devices), this concentration results in a more traditional product range. It is precisely the relatively advanced technology products that are given up.

(2) The functional repertoire of the plants of the Western corporations is of crucial importance for the host economy's potential to generate entrepreneurship. A lack of decision-making corporate functions, especially those of qualified engineering and management functions, is also a lack of those 'seed beds' that produce entrepreneurs. Moreover, a lack of these functions hinders the development of a significant regional middle class and the 'culture and society' associated with this strata. The non-generation of any real middle-class and their associated culture, however, would reinforce the difficulties in attracting the upper echelon of technical and managerial staff to other regional firms - a disastrous circle.

(3) The type of work organization employed in the plants of the large Western corporations has also considerable consequences for the potential to generate entrepreneurship. Whereas mass assembly does not favour a type of work organization that

stimulates those social competencies that are the main ingredient of entrepreneurship, customized production calls for a broad range of skills and fluid job demarcations, which stimulate social competencies, such as self-reliance and the ability to co-operate.

(4) The size of a plant influences the potential to induce spin-offs and entrepreneurs. Empirical material suggests that smaller plants are more conducive to the generation of entrepreneurship than larger ones.

(5) So far, the disastrous economic situation of the Central and Eastern European countries has forced them into tough competition for Western investors which regularly results in an extensive exemption from obligations concerning linkages to the pre-existing production system or from the stimulation of entrepreneurship (broad functional repertoire, flexible work organization, small plant size). As is well established in the literature, the large corporations increasingly reduce the share of in-house production in order to deal with the high demands for flexibility. Such a strategy to externalize risks, however, presupposes reliable and responsive - which usually means nearby - subcontracting networks. Therefore, at least the Western investors with a long-term perspective in Central and Eastern Europe, cannot be

interested in the complete marginalization of their host economies. The RDA could play a central role in the 'embedding' of the Western corporations. On the one hand, they could provide information on potential suppliers to Western investors, on the other hand, they could assist the these suppliers in upgrading their technical and organizational know-how. Without such attempts to embed the plants of the Western corporations, they will remain 'cathedrals in the desert'. This, however, would inevitably result in a polarization between a few Western enclaves and marginalized regional economies.

5.4. Regional Financial Organization

It has already been suggested above that the financial system be formed around a system of trade and development banks aimed at providing the possibility for individuals to act as market-makers, using banks to finance positions in goods which are being moved either geographically or temporally. Certain types of financial vehicles, such as trade bills, could then be used to finance the work in process of manufacturing firms and agricutural enterprises. In this way, market based exchange creates the asset which can provide the basis for lending by the banks. It is clear that banks will acquire and also require the same type of information which is vested in the Regional Development Associations (see above). This suggests that there should either be close co-operation between the trade and development banks and the Associations, or that the government should charge the Associations with the operation of Regional Development Banks operated through branches at the local level.

This approach would borrow from another aspect of the German financial system whereby the savings banks regulated at the regional level are joined together into national clearing houses or "Girozentralen". In this way, the local banks can provide for their clients' access to all aspects of financing and economies of scale which would not be possible for any single bank acting on its own. It is thus possible to conserve both the local control and direct knowledge of its clients associated with small unit bank systems, strongly defended in the US, and the economies and range of action associated with the large banks operating without restriction across all types of financial activity. There is no presumption that the local banks need necessarily be government owned (although this may be necessary initially), but that they should be linked to, and their information coordinated with, the Development councils.

6. MAKING THE INTERNATIONAL CONTEXT

None of the Eastern European economies or the newly formed economies of the former USSR can achieve transformation without extensive international co-operation. They will not only rely on exchanges of goods and services with other economies; as long as the modernization and expansion cannot be funded exclusively from internal savings, the import of foreign capital, financial as well as human, will be necessary. By 1992 it is clear that not only the old nation States such as Hungary, Poland or Czechoslovakia will have their own currencies, but so will the new independent republics which are emerging from the former Soviet Union and Yugoslavia. There is imminent danger that the old production and exchange structure will be discontinued, not only between former CMEA countries, but also between the new States. The economic history of post-World-War-I

Europe, and in particular of the successor States of the Austro-Hungarian Empire, provides one possible result of such action. The danger connected with liberalized, i.e. unregulated, trade between the former Republics of the Soviet Union and Yugoslavia as between all former CMEA countries calls for urgent action to revitalize multilateral trade and economic co-operation at all levels.

There is no doubt that action on the 'intra-regional' as well as on the international level is necessary. The utility of preserving intra-regional trade via a regional East European Payments Union or a free trade area has already been mentioned. The equivalent structure at the international level involves a payments or clearing union which would ensure an equitable division of the burden of transition between the surplus countries of the industrialized world and the formerly planned economies of Central and Eastern Europe.

6.1. The National and the Multilateral Levels

Since it is unlikely that internal accumulation through domestic savings will be sufficient to bring about the changes in the methods of production and the quality of goods which will be necessary to achieve what has been called the 'internal' or 'commodity' convertibility of the currency, i.e., the voluntary preference of residents for domestic goods when they are available, foreign lending will be necessary. If 'internal' accumulation is insufficient to guarantee 'internal' convertibility, it will certainly not allow 'external' convertibility, which provides for non-residents voluntarily preferring Eastern European goods to domestic production. As a rule, deficits on current account will be a part of the transformation process and they will have to be financed by voluntary capital inflows or by policies to restrict domestic demand and output, making transformation that much more difficult. The current fashionable 'big bang' approach relies on a sufficiently large devaluation to produce an export surplus, and a sufficiently drastic cut in real wages and government expenditures to reduce inflation so as to produce conditions compatible with convertibility at a fixed rate of exchange. However, if output falls more rapidly than the reduction in demand as real wages and government expenditures are cut, it becomes particularly difficult for those countries which have decided on fixed rate convertibility to maintain exchange rates without falling into the trap of overvalued domestic currencies or rapidly diminishing undervaluation, which encourages imports and penalizes exports. Under such conditions the external constraint quickly reappears and policy makers are confronted with the choice between even more restrictive domestic demand policies, aggravating the already steep falls in production, the loss of exchange reserves and eventual devaluation, undermining the credibility of the attempt to introduce fixed rate convertibility, or a rapid devaluation which may evoke the 'vicious circle' of inflation, rising unemployment and devaluation. Indeed, in those countries currently experimenting with the 'big bang', the 'stop-go' policy cycle in vicious circle conditions of stagflation and further devaluation seems to have taken hold before reconstruction has had time to occur and seems to make it even more difficult to achieve.

Thus, the need for an automatic international mechanism of finance such as might be found in an international clearing union. Therefore, we argue in favour of the institution of both an international and a regional payments union. But there is an additional reason for these institutions, which deals with the problem of the risk of foreign investment in the formerly planned economies. In the absence of internal accumulation capable of producing either internal or external convertibility, steps will have to be taken to provide for access to foreign capital and the foreign technology necessary to guarantee an output which meets international competitive standards. Any voluntary private foreign investment will require not only the right to profit repatriation, but also a reasonable expectation of exchange rate stability.

No matter how difficult convertibility is to achieve, it remains a key factor in attracting the foreign investment required for successful transformation. The basic difficulty with fixed-rate convertibility for a formerly planned economy with limited foreign exchange reserves is that it has to be guaranteed by a single institution, its Central Bank, without the help of an international lender of last resort unless it wants to submit its reconstruction programme to the control of foreign governments or international agencies. But, there may be an alternative to this domestic (or 'private') assurance of convertibility: public assurance. Just as a country's 'public' Central Bank provides lender of last resort support to 'private' commercial banks to allow them to guarantee that the private liabilities they issue in the form of bank deposits will have a permanent 1:1 parity with the Central Bank's public liabilities represented by the note issue or money base, the same sort of guarantees could be provided for a single country's currency on an international level by a centralized clearing house for external payments.

Keynes' proposal for a Clearing Union may also be viewed as a way of providing financing for countries wishing to expand internal demand in excess of domestic resources for the purpose of reconstruction without forcing them on the mercy of the liquidity preference of the financial asset holders of the surplus countries and to introduce restrictive policies to assure currency convertibility. In this interpretation the role of the Clearing Union is to act just like any other financial intermediary, interfacing between the liquidity requirements of surplus country private creditors and the financing requirements of deficit country debtors. Instead of intermediating between short and long maturity assets, its main function is to intermediate between assets denominated in surplus and deficit country currencies. Under a Clearing Union, it would be as if the Central Bank of the surplus country investor, rather than the private residents of the surplus country, became the primary creditor of the deficit country through its credit balances with the Clearing Union, which it finances by issuing domestic currency assets to private holders. It is not a question of whether foreign lending will take place - if reconstruction is to succeed it has to. The problem is to try to reduce the risk of devaluation to the lender by creating an international intermediary which will bear the currency risk of immediate convertibility. In this way, the Clearing Union eliminates the necessity of a small country attempting the contradictory policy of expanding by means of a contractionary fiscal policy which generates a current account surplus, or a monetary policy which is more restrictive than the surplus country in order to attract capital inflows to offset a current account deficit. In this way, each country which runs a surplus trade balance with an economy undergoing transition automatically provides the lending necessary to support it. Looked at another way, each individual, developed country government is providing an exchange guarantee to its exporters and to its residents who are investing in the process of transition. If there is some resistance to an international agency, such as the formal Clearing Union, the same result could be accomplished by each Western government providing exchange rate guarantees to its residents who invest in an Eastern European country in much the same way so that insurance and subsidized finance are provided in the form of export credits to domestic exporters. It makes little difference if the industrialized governments undertake this themselves, or if they act through private markets via foreign exchange futures and options markets. It would seem preferable to introduce exchange rate subsidies for capital investors, rather than granting funds for exchange stabilization by the individual central banks, and thereby running the risk that the funds will simply be used to finance luxury imports or foreign travel.

However this scheme is arranged, some type of international intermediation or national support of formerly planned economy direct investment will be necessary in order to encourage the capital flows required for rapid reconstruction. The use of an international asset which is non-negotiable except for the settlement of international payments and issued by the Union removes the private risk of holding the debts of deficit countries, and transfers it to the world economy as a whole and to the Central Bank of the creditor countries in particular. In such a system a small country need not provide private guarantees of convertibility and may thus avoid trying to combine full employment policy with convertibility. Thus, it seems that the most appropriate way of assuring some semblance of external convertibility would be to recognize that instant introduction of free multilateral trade and convertibility is inimical to reconstruction and that the most sensible approach would be through the introduction of an International Clearing Union.

The introduction of a free trade area along with a clearing union among the former Eastern European CMEA countries would also fit into the apparent strategy of the EEC's concept of a European Economic Area, which has just granted to the EFTA countries most of the privileges of membership without requiring formal membership and financial contribution. This also extends to membership in the EMS. All of this is, of course, politically difficult, for it requires the recognition that there is no easy instant introduction of the 'market' and that a 'third way' must be found if chaos is to be avoided. It also requires voluntary co-operation amongst countries which have just managed to gain individual freedom of action, however limited by economic constraints. There is no question that the successor States to the Soviet Union should be full and active members of any association or union. Given their natural resource position, the countries succeeding the former USSR will clearly, on the whole, be giving as much as they would be getting from entering such an alliance on an equal basis. The United States has learned in recent years that increasing international economic integration has limited both its international economic and political power, as well as its ability to act independently of the other industrialized economies. This is a lesson which proud leaders in countries with newly won democracy and independence must also learn. If not, the gains in democracy now in place will quickly give way to more authoritarian, and more nationalist forms of centralized government. Excesses like those of the reactions to both Weimar and the '29 Crash could be avoided as the former socialist command economies worked their way towards what history tells us must be a 'third way'.

6.2. The Task of the Surplus Countries

There is no way to balance trade between the former centrally planned and the hard currency countries except by squeezing internal demand to an extent that hampers production and investment. High investment needed for modernization and expansion of output therefore necessarily goes together with a deficit in the current account. It would have to be financed by capital imports, if socio-economic reconstruction is not to be impeded. The task of the hard currency countries, in particular the EEC-countries, the USA and Japan would be threefold:

First, to abolish trade barriers impeding import from the former centrally planned countries, as this would allow the transformation economies to pay an increasing amount of import by their own exports.

Second, to establish a Central and Eastern European Recovery Programme which takes up the lessons of the post World War II years in Central and Eastern Europe. Over a period of five years, finance should be allocated to exchange rate guarantees for capital exports to the transformation countries, or to support the regional payments union. The counterpart in domestic currency should be paid into a Socio-economic Reconstruction Fund in each receiver country.

Third, to make access to these funds conditional. Next to observing universal human rights, two economic conditions should be made mandatory: the establishment of a socio-economic reconstruction programme in co-operation with the donor countries, as well as the effective co-operation in the establishment and operation of both the Clearing Union which encompasses the former CMEA-region and the one which, in addition, includes the developed industrial countries within OECD. An additional source of capital for the Socio-Economic Reconstruction Fund could be found in the purchase of (tactical) nuclear weapons especially by NATO for the purpose of dismantling them. The co-operation should, finally, also be extended to a mutual exchange programme of experts in management, administration and research, as well as industries.

7. THE AGENDA

Mature market economies which former communist countries in Central and Eastern Europe want to copy are, of course, the result of an evolution over centuries. Since Karl Polanyi's oeuvre this process has been known as 'The Great Transformation'. The new rulers and their Western advisers appear to impose the task of repeating the Great Transformation in a 'Big Leap Forward' on the people in the former command economies. This time it is called 'Shock Therapy' or 'Big Bang'. By 1992, the contention that the new 'Big Leap Forward' will anew end in disaster has become certainty. The increasing weaknesses of the economies to be transformed are now apparent. In none of the transformation economies the decline of production, investment and employment has come to a halt or has been reversed.

The October Revolution of 1917 proved that communism can neither be established by revolution nor by decree. The years 1989 and after have so far shown that neither a capitalist market economy can be introduced by decree alone.

It is now clear that political changes in Eastern Europe are so permanent and far-reaching that a return to communist rule and a command economic system is no longer a credible threat, but has become a ghost without any chance of reincarnation. As in the 1930's, the greater threat menaces democracy from a rather different direction. An important justification for the economic crash programmes of unrestrained economic liberalization - destroying the road back to communism - no longer exists. Therefore, it is important to evaluate the transformation strategies hitherto pursued. They are all descendants of what is known as 'IMF-conditionality' mandated for extending IMF and World Bank loans to capitalist market economies with weak currencies, most of them developing economies in the Third World.

As a first step, the evaluation should try to emphasize the strengths and weaknesses of the conventional transformation strategies. Next, elements should be presented to be seriously considered for inclusion in a programme aimed at socio-economic reconstruction. This is the motivation behind this AGENDA. There is no doubt that a concrete AGENDA for each single country can never be worked out by absentee-thinkers in Washington D.C.,

Bonn, Brussels or at centres of intellectual excellence such as Harvard, nor by a multinational and multidisciplinary working group like the one which volunteered for this AGENDA. The subsequent arguments are presented in such a spirit. They summarize sections 1 to 6 above and are intended as a kind of check list for the building of transformation programmes.

7.1. Why Conventional Transformation Strategies for Transformation Fail

The principal merit of the conventional transformation strategy in its various forms is the rejection of the idea of central planning and its replacement by a system of decentralized initiatives of economic agents. The conventional strategy includes additional elements such as the role of private property in the form of entitlement of private principals and agents in production, distribution and finance, the coordination of private, decentralized initiatives by markets, the rollback of State intervention and regulation of economic activities, the emphasis on monetary stability and on relative prices. There is wide agreement on the principal merits of a system of decentralized initiatives and of the potential usefulness of elements just mentioned. They are widely accepted as necessary ingredients, and this view is also shared by the AGENDA-Group.

Why then can IMF-inspired programmes be judged to be failures? Of course, the most important criterion is to be seen in their concrete results. However, the gap between promise and outcome may, to a great extent, be simply due to errors, mistakes, shortcomings, omissions and misconceptions which then affect the concrete programmes and their implementation.

The *main error* lies in the belief in the spontaneous appearance of a capitalist market economy once private property is established, prices are set free, currency is stabilized and unregulated competitive markets are introduced. This 'error of spontaneity' creates serious shortcomings. First, it does not recognize the fact that markets are a social construction which have to be created by human action. This was already described in detail by representatives of the Austrian School of Economics at the turn of the century. Ronald Coase, the Nobel-Prize winner in 1991, explicitely states that the markets must be made - as it has already been the case. This is a genuine entrepreneurial task. In these cases where markets do not emerge by spontaneous entrepreneurial action, they have to be established by conscious public, or if necessary, by state action. This is one of AGENDA's crucial conclusions. The 'error of spontaneity' from which all conventional transformation strategies so far pursued suffer leads to policies which propose the creation of 'markets' without the least concern for the creation of 'market-makers'.

In capitalist market economies, the market-maker may be idealized in the 'middleman', who establishes contacts between production units in agriculture and industry and final buyers whose operations are closely linked to the existence of financing from commercial bankers. Both the market-maker and the banker establish contracts in which money is credited to the producing (or distributing) agent in exchange for the promise of repayment plus interest. This creates the necessity for monitoring contract performance by both. This is also the source of what is called the 'hard budget constraint': the necessity of repaying loans at interest with the money proceeds gained from the sale of outputs in free, competitive markets. These contracts establish the market in which production and distribution can take place. The market in which a credit-production-distribution and a credit-investment-process can take place does not emerge spontaneously.

Capitalist markets are caracterized by their capacity to induce economic agents to crate *additional* output and value. This is essentially what the peoples of the former Soviet Empire expect when they support the transformation of the command to the capitalist market economies. The road to capitalism, as experienced until now, did, however, only introduce markets for the exchange of already existing goods and values. To a great extent, these have been exchanged for speculative purposes only, without creating incentives for the production and investment process.

Equally serious is the neglect of the socio-economic context as a necessary precondition of production and distribution of already existing wealth and, along with it, the creation and distribution of new wealth. These issues remain completely outside the scope of IMF-inspired programmes.

The *main mistake* is that IMF-type programmes give more weight to three single measures: (1) The stabilization of the currency, (2) price deregulation as well as elimination of State intervention and (3) privatization. Their immediate and radical implementation has not halted the fall in production and employment. It is a serious mistake to believe that a set of three measures alone can create a socio-economic context in which the single agents, by the pursuit of their private interest, add to their own benefit and to that of the whole society. On the contrary, 'shock therapy' adds more damage to the socio-economic context that already exists. While reducing output and employment, such a transformation strategy sets the stage for a negative-sum game in which private gain tends to contribute to the decrease in output. The making of a socio-economic context promoting socio-economic reconstruction is - as was first stressed by Adam Smith - the genuine task and responsibility of the law maker. Spontaneity cannot be expected to put an end to the negative-sum or zero-sum game.

The *main shortcomings*: Of a number of shortcomings which result from a strategy in which there is no place for either market-makers or the context makers, five arc discussed here because of their importance to AGENDA:

1) Immediate privatization of state enterprises (a kind of 'forced privatization') is detrimental to the necessary improvement of production. It is a disincentive to managers before actual privatization occurs. It may not even stimulate production afterwards, as the new owners may prefer to speculate by hoarding resources (e. g. land). Given present circumstances this aggravates the crisis of the production system.

2) Freeing of prices in current conditions of massive imbalance is not likely to stimulate output and distribution of goods and services. In the absence of a credible currency, this only tends to make financial speculation more attractive and does not contribute at all to the creation of new wealth.

3) Stabilization programmes disregard the asyncrony between restructuring the supply side and the reduction of the demand overhang. It also disregards the fact that stabilization policies usually tend to reduce supply. Thus imbalances may not be reduced, but simply reappear at a different level. The historical experience of IMF-type stabilization programmes suggest that they provide no guarantee that successful economic stabilization will automatically lead to a resumption of sustained economic growth.

4) The introduction of convertibility in the old and new States of the former CMEA-area would intensify the constraint on output by increasing prices of imports needed as inputs in the production process. In addition most traditional markets will be lost as soon as exports have to be paid in hard currency.

5) The role of the State in economic and social affairs is basically restricted to legislation concerning privatization, monetary reform and price deregulation on the one hand and to reducing public expenditures on the other.

7.2. Neglect of Historical Experiences

In fact, the historical experiences of the 'economic miracles' of post-war reconstruction in Western Europe expressly contradict the belief in a spontaneaous short cut leading to the high road to capitalism. During the period of reconstruction 1) exchange rates were managed, capital flows were strictly regulated and convertibility for commercial transactions was introduced over a period of ten years; 2) controls and subsidies on prices of key commodities were maintained over the same extended period, and in some cases, controls and subsidies (e. g. in agriculture and energy) are still applied; 3) privatization was never given a high priority and many successful companies (e. g. Volkswagenwerke) have not profited from the benefits of private ownership for decades without any visible detriment to their performance; 4) international exchange was managed by means of a well designed scheme, the European Payments Union, with the aim of restoring multilateral trade amongst the OEEC countries by loosening the constraint ot the scarcity of dollars; 5) rational economic planning and national economic accounting were put into place, aided by the Marshall Plan, to provide for the reconstruction of the necessary infrastructure and key sectors of industry in the order they were needed to ensure balanced recovery;

6) financial and technical support from the USA under the Marshall Plan was conditional to points 4) and 5) and US experts both supported and controlled these activities; 7) monetary and fiscal reforms and stabilization policies were clearly regarded as instrumental to the reconstruction and expansion of the productive system; by no means was the realization of abstract monetary targets allowed to lead to the destruction of productive assets; 8) an active State, capable of governing and supporting the market through the creation of institutions, the legal structures, as well as taxation and expenditure programmes, was a key factor in enhancing the economic environment for entrepreneurial activities.

An important historical lesson may also be drawn from the successful modernization and expansion of the Japanese economy; and, subsequently, of the so-called 'Little Tigers': Hong Kong, Taiwan, Singapore, and South Korea. Their success is based upon an undogmatic recognition that markets must be governed in order to provide support for entrepreneurial initiatives undertaken at government suggestion. None of the 'economic miracles' which have been achieved in these countries could have been attained by following the short cut to capitalism mapped out for the former command economies of Eastern Europe.

7.3. Main Topics in AGENDA

An AGENDA cannot be built on caveats, it calls for arguments in support of active policy. This AGENDA's guiding principle is its concern for socio-economic reconstruction and growth of output, employment and welfare. This objective requires conscious action by individuals, single agents, collective actors and public authority. These actions should be stimulated and coordinated by a socio-economic context in which the pursuit of individual interest adds both to individual and to social welfare. Such a context is made up of market forces supported by appropriate institutions (including forms of property and contracts) and guided by appropriate policies, all being supporting instruments. They cannot, however, be ends in themselves. These guiding principles should be reflected in the list and contents of the topics of any AGENDA which is concerned with the road to create new value in the former communist countries.

Topic 1: Stabilizing output and employment
The decline of domestic production has to be stopped. Privatization of State property should be restricted to cases where output can be stabilized. Privatization of the management of State firms should be given priority. The reward system should be linked to the expansion of sale

of output and to the increase of productive assets. Privatization of public property should, as a rule, be postponed until management and other domestic groups are in a position to buy, or to manage on the behalf of others, productive assets. The immediate problem of human suffering - unemployment, reduction in living standards, social dislocation - must be dealt with on a priority basis. Shock therapy on its own, or other social experiments in the name of a better future, cannot be acceptable, if this brings about present economic disaster and political disorder.

As no civilized society can withhold the basic necessities of life to the unemployed, old, sick or disabled, these resources should be made available on a rational basis. Wherever possible, social benefits should be made available in a way that is conducive to socio-economic reconstruction. This refers in particular to the unemployed. Their social income should be geared to programmes of retraining and training. Schemes including laboratory-type establishments should guarantee basic provision plus a premium in exchange for the acquisition of skills needed in the transformation process and also for the creation of product ideas with a potentially high demand. It is an important lesson learned from periods of acute shortage and famine that free distribution of aid cannot resolve the problem. Even in these cases schemes should be preferred in which the participants of the workforce are only entitled to aid in exchange for payment and participation in public works if they are out of work. It is essential that everyone contributes to production and that the burden of the transition is shared equitably. Otherwise there will be not even a minimum social consensus without which successful reconstruction is hardly attainable.

Topic 2: Making the Context for Growth of Production

The essence of a market economy is the action of productive and distributive agents to increase future output and incomes. It is based on contracts which relate present input to future output and reward. Finance - private and loan capital - is a necessary condition for production and distribution in markets. Making the context for growth of production therefore requires at least:

(1) a currency sufficiently stable to act as the appropriate unit in which to denominate future contracts and assets serving as collateral;

(2) the enforcement of money contracts;

(3) the private management of (public) firms where managers are accountable for results and paid according to performance;

(4) the 'middle man' who provides the market linkage of production units with buying units (the wholesalers, or the sales division in a company as well as the commercial and investment bank extending loans to the producing or distributing agents in exchange for repayment and interest);

(5) a mildly expansive monetary and fiscal policy which allows output to grow by providing sufficient effective demand;

(6) incomes policies organized by trade unions and business organizations supporting the socio-economic reconstruction.

There is no urgent need for full scale privatization of productive assets, for the freeing of prices and incomes, for introducing full scale convertibility, for establishing stock and foreign exchanges. All these characteristics of pure market economies are not fully realized in any existing Western economy. They should only be introduced if they provide stimulation of production and a reduction of imbalances. Capitalism requires institutions which guarantee that undertaking permanent business relations and the associated investment of capital earn positive net returns. A deregulated form of capitalism bare of appropriate institutions is not able to produce the wealth expected by the citizens of the former communist countries

- it becomes nothing more than a casino which takes bets on the value of existing physical objects.

Topic 3: Industrial and Regional Policies

In the history of capitalist development 'latecomers' have not relied on the spontaneous market forces. Higher efforts and lower prices help to to reduce the competitive gap; however, they are not sufficient to 'catch up'. Cases in point are Japan and the 'Little Tigers' to mention recent examples, and the war-stricken countries in OEEC Europe after World War II. Industrial and regional policies were designed to promote the production of import substitutes and exportable output. Successful examples suggest that industrial and regional policy programmes are necessary parts of any strategy which does not rely on a belief in a spontaneous socio-economic reconstruction. There is an existing industrial basis and a pattern of specialization in most areas of Central and Eastern Europe. Notwithstanding the fact that both reflect all the severe deficiencies of the collapsed system of central planning and communist dictatorship, they can and must serve as a starting point for regional and industrial policy. In the necessary process of reconstruction drastic changes occur and will continue to do so. If full collapse of the economy is to be prevented, restructuring has to take place under selective protection. Protection is necessary in order to give potentially competitive producers a chance to adjust to the new conditions. Competitive adjustments have to be based on innovative potentials of engineers, craftsmen, organizers as well as on supply and sales networks. As these are often, especially in transition periods, regarded as 'mere cost factors' and not as potential innovation factors, they have also to be protected against simple-minded cost-cutting. Industrial and regional development in the post-communist countries do not represent a context where one can simply rely on the 'market' to provide the optimum solution. In this area, functioning markets and capable agents cannot be expected to spring up like mushrooms after the rain of privatization; they have to be created by conscious institutional design and public policies.

Obviously, there will be objections that these proposals involve the reintroduction of planning. This is not to be denied. The successsful operation and expenditure of Marshall Plan funds was based on national accounting and economic planning. Similarly, the successful operation of any capitalist firm is based on strategic planning within a market system. The benefits of free market competition come only at the cost of an increasingly uncertain future economic environment. The only way to take rational decisions in this environment is to try to foresee future eventualities. In a market system, planning is being prepared for every future eventuality. In command economies, planning failed for various reasons: one is that the mere existence of a plan cannot make the future certain. The transforming economies will only succeed in the international market economy if they learn to use rational planning as an instrument of free choice and decision making.

Topic 4: The International Context

At present, economic agents in the former communist countries are not fit for unrestrained competition in the world markets. The process of socio-economic reconstruction has to be sheltered, if it is to take place at all. The decrease in protection is an important instrument in stimulating the process. The removal of protective measures can only be a long-term objective. In OECD countries, basic characteristics of trade liberalization and full convertibility were realized only within the last two decades and the process has not yet come to an end. Measures to be included in AGENDA therefore comprise the following:

(1) Convertibility of the domestic currency into hard currency should be reserved for productive agents; it is to be regulated for consumption purposes.

(2) A Payments Union should be established between the old and new States of the former CMEA area. Its purpose is to settle the bilateral balances between single members of the Union multilaterally. This would allow continued deliveries to honour contracts established under the old CMEA regime. It would also enable the settlement of imbalances without recourse to loans and restriction of output. This is an important contribution to Topic 1: Stabilizing Output and Employment, as there do not exist immediate substitutes for the former CMEA markets in hard currency areas.

(3) There remain important tasks for the hard currency surplus countries in the OECD world. First, these countries should increase their imports from transforming countries which are becoming competitive. This would allow export revenues to grow. Secondly, capital exports from the surplus countries to the transformation countries should be increased. Private capital exports should be accompanied by a Central and Eastern European Recovery Programme - inspired by the successful post-World War II European Reconstruction Programme - which also would add to their success. Financial resources would have to be provided by multinational and supranational bodies and paid by

their member States. Over a period of five years, funds should be allocated to transformation countries annually with the purpose of financing exchange rate guarantees for capital imports earmarked for socio-economic reconstruction programmes. In each receiver country, the equivalent in domestic currency should be paid into a Socio-Economic Reconstruction Fund. The access to these funds would have to be made conditional. Apart from the observation of universal human rights two conditions are topical: the establishment of a national socio-economic reconstruction programme in co-operation with the donor countries as well as the effective co-operation in the establishment and operation of the multilateral settlement scheme between the States in the transformation area. Additional capital for the Central and Eastern European Reconstruction Fund could be raised, if NATO bought nuclear weapons for the purpose of dismantling them. This would be a measure which is - as is demonstrated now - much cheaper than the humanitarian or peace keeping actions which ensue from the wars emerging in the absence of serious socio-economic reconstruction. (By August 1992, this proposal is already knowledge founded by historical experience). Finally, the co-operation scheme should also include a mutual exchange programme for experts in industries, services, in public administration and research: it should encompass all levels of competence and hierarchy.

Topic 5: The Role of the State

A project of socio-economic reconstruction which does not rely on spontaneity as the key organizing principle requires an active State. Its tasks are manifold: it has to create the institutions and the legal framework which support socio-economic reconstruction; to introduce monetary and fiscal reforms and policies of promotion of industries, regions and exports; of selective protectionism and of skill promotion, to mention only some important examples. Above all, the active role of the State is a condition for the staging of a socio-economic context, in which the participation of individuals and social groups in the socio-economic reconstruction occurs in pursuit of their self-interest. This includes the making of functioning markets as a crucial part of the socio-economic context; a task which, to stress it once more, cannot be left to spontaneous individual action. In the socio-economic reconstruction project, the State has the task of reconciling private and public interests. This is the classical role ascribed to the State by Adam Smith. The State as 'the invisible hand' precludes those results of self-interested action that are incompatible with social welfare.

By their very nature, transitional economies have weak governments of limited jurisdiction and administrative capabilities. Policies must be tailored to this reality. A means of giving more administrative capacities to a weak State is to pursue policies that build bridges between the different social classes by seeking consensus. Policies that encourage social co-operation rather than conflict therefore need to be favoured in general, in so far as they do not jeopardize socio-economic reconstruction. Social co-operation rests on collective actors who organize individual interest. Trade unions, federations of industrialists, crafts associations and other business organizations are therefore indispensable partners in a social game which aims at arriving at a social consensus for social reconstruction. Contrary to the world view of underlying IMF-type transformation programmes, this AGENDA considers collective actors, if legitimized by their members, as potentially highly productive, organizing factors in modern industrial societies.

7.4. Outlook

The most important single factor for social and economic recovery is a common, shared World View which supports socio-economic reconstruction. A project widely associated with structural change, modernization and growth, brought about by personal initiative anchored in the minds and personal interests of the people creates a climate in which social interaction takes place with a moderate level of coordination. It is not difficult then to have public authority accepted, if it is exercised according to these common perceptions. The same is true with respect to the role of the State. After World War II, such a social partnership emerged in some of the most successful democracies in Western Europe. The post-communist societies have a long way to go to reach such a state of affairs and some are even moving in the opposite direction. The old certainties and uncertainties of the centrally planned economies have disappeared only to be replaced by the new uncertainties of a still only hoped for market economy. The consequences are what one can call 'interaction crisis'. Public authority in affairs dealing with everyday life, with private and professional life, is very low. The government and public administration are far from having control over their own domains, which are often not yet clearly defined. The purposefulness and the enforcement of public action have collapsed together with the rule of the communist party which, in the old regime, acted as both a steering wheel and a driving force. In 1992, the interaction crisis will probably come close to chaos in some post-communist countries, with all the risks involved. The emergence of dictatorship, the intensification of ethnic conflicts and even more open wars cannot be ruled out. The seductive promises of the authoritarian State will again make it a real threat. There is an important lesson from recent communist dictatorships that should not be forgotten. The authoritarian State is not able to cope with the problems discussed here. Socio-economic reconstruction calls for the strength of a democratic State capable of inspiring its citizens to self-interested voluntary co-operation.

What will the chances be for a project of socio-economic reconstruction which is buildt on the principles and arguments suggested by this AGENDA? It is understandable that there is a longing for cohesion by those living in countries in continuous unrest near to chaos. A popular strategy to unite a nation is to fight an external enemy, which is rather easy to create. Uniting the people in a constructive project is much more difficult. The first difficulty is its elaboration. The second difficulty lies in the organization of a social consensus for its implementation. The purpose of this AGENDA is to provide an argument for coping with these difficulties.

APPENDIX

DOCUMENTATION OF BACKGROUND PAPERS

1. Asztalos, L.G.:
   Interaction of Politics and Economics in the Process of the Hungarian Transformation.

2. Bayer, K.:
   Structural Change.

3. Bhaduri, A.:
   IMF-style Stabilization.

4. Bhaduri, A./Matzner, E.:
   Proposal for an Urgent Elaboration of an Agenda for Socio-Economic Reconstruciton of Central and Eastern European Countries (AGENDA).

5. Grabher, G.:
   Re-Creating Regional Economies in Eastern Europe.

6. Herr, H.:
   Two Views on How a Market Economy Functions.

7. Herr, H./Tober, S.:
   A Strategy for Economic Transformation and Development.

8. Kalmbach, B.:
   Market Forces and Industrial Policy in the Process of Transition in the Eastern Economies.

9. Kolloch, E.:
   East European Indebtedness - New Financial Constraints.

10. Komarek, V.:
    Macro-economic Conditions of Economic Reform: The Case of CSFR.

11. Kregel, J.A.:
    International Financial Constraints.

12. Kregel, J.A.:
    Preparatory Document for AGENDA Drafting Session

13. Lushin, A.S.:
    The External Opening of Transforming Economy: The Case of Russia.

14. Matzner, E.:
    Main Issues in an AGENDA for Socio-Economic Reconstruction of Central and Eastern European Countries.

15. Matzner, E.:
    AGENDA (first and second Draft)

16. Perczynski, M.:
    Subregional Co-operation in Eastern and Central Europe in the Period of Systemic Transformation.

17. Schmidt, M.:
    East German Experience for a Strategy of Economic Transformation.

18. Specht, L.:
    The Politics of Property

19. Unger, R. M.:
    Political Economy After Communism and Neo-Liberalism: The Better Futures of the Peripheral Economies

20. Smirnova, S.A.:
    Privatization in Russia: Socio-Economic Context and Structural Issues.